T0082876

A Life on God's Terms

Responding to God's Love in Loving Abandon

TWILA JENSEN

WESTBOW PRESS®
A DIVISION OF THOMAS NELSON & ZONDERVAN

WestBow Press books may be ordered through booksellers or by contacting:

WestBow Press
A Division of Thomas Nelson & Zondervan
1663 Liberty Drive
Bloomington, IN 47403
www.westbowpress.com
1 (866) 928-1240

ISBN: 978-1-9736-1905-5 (sc)
ISBN: 978-1-9736-1904-8 (e)

Print information available on the last page.

WestBow Press rev. date: 02/09/2018

Dedication

I dedicate this book to Dave Lowe who has been a wonderful boss, friend, mentor and inspiration to me. Your encouragement and belief in me has meant more than you know. I wouldn't be where I am in life without your influence.

I dedicate this book to my husband Michael who is my daily encouragement and support. I also dedicate this book to my boys Travis, Thomas, and Carter who are a constant joy.

I dedicate this book to my mother, Dave Johnson and Susan Sievers who gave me a strong foundation in Christ which I am ever grateful for.

Contents

Seize Life!

Seize life! Eat bread with gusto,
Drink wine with a robust heart.
Oh yes—God takes pleasure in your pleasure!
Dress festively every morning.
Don't skimp on colors and scarves.
Relish life with the spouse you love
Each and every day of your precarious life.
Each day is God's gift. It's all you get in exchange
For the hard work of staying alive.
Make the most of each one!
Whatever turns up, grab it and do it. And heartily!
This is your last and only chance at it.
(Ecclesiastes 9:7-9, MSG)

The Treasure Hunt

The Hidden Matzah is Always Found by the Children

At a Jewish Seder in celebration of Passover, the leader of the family performs the *yachatz* ceremony, breaking the middle matzah into two unequal parts. The smaller part is put back into its original position and the other part is hidden for the children to find. This unleavened bread, pierced through with holes, is known as "the bread of affliction." The children are charged with finding this hidden treasure. Once they find it, they eat of it in silence before midnight.

Life is a hidden treasure for the heart of the child to find. It is in finding Jesus, our bread of life, who was pierced through for our transgressions, that we savor the goodness that is right before us. Jesus is the bread of life. It is only by Him and in Him that we find our life.

Sometimes we can go through the motions or work hard to try to get everything right in our faith walk and we fail to see the hidden manna right before us. He offers it freely to us, not if we get it all right, but just as we are.

When I was a new Christian, I used to think God somehow judged me based on my performance as a Christian. I continually felt frustrated in my walk with Him because I could not seem to get my act together. I saw Him as angry and felt distant. During this time, I felt prompted to write this conversational poem–

A Conversation with God: A Love So Divine

Precious Daughter, don't you know,
How it is I love you so?
You are my daughter, created with much thought,
Just perfect for the purpose which you are sought.
I will be there to guide the way,
To hold you, teach you, and protect you from stray.
Just hold out your hand and trust in me,
Then my dear, wait and see.
Let go of the striving and trying to please,
You desire approval to feel at ease.
Your security is held tight in my hand,
As I've promised you, Twila, the Promised Land.

Yes, of course I call you by name,
You're uniquely separate and not the same.
Learn to be who you are,
With your own special gifts step out and apart.
Trust in my Word as I speak to you,
Remember that I will see you through.
Don't let fear keep you away,
From all I have for you each day.
You are special in my eyes and I do care,
No matter the problem, I will be there.

Even when I stray so far, even when I pull apart?
Will you still love me, will you still care?
Can I count on you to be there??
With all this striving, I get so lost,
I sin against you at such a high cost.
I push you away and go my own way,
I feel so lost when my heart goes astray.
Your love is what I really need,
Your approval, to know that You are pleased.
To feel your heart beat with mine,
To be wrapped in Your love that is so divine.

Precious daughter, as you well know,
I care for you and love you so.
I watch over you all your days,
Leading and guiding you in my ways.
I am not angry at you,
I love to see all that you do.
Learning to obey won't happen in one day,
So let me wash your frets away.
You will get there in My time,
Let go into My love that is so divine!

We all have weaknesses and imperfections. God, in His endless grace, is not trying to make us perfect, but to show us our deeper need for a Savior. As we see our need and inability to live out our lives according to God's Word and guidance in our own strength, we are driven to Him.

Coming as a child in need of saving, humble and dependent, we find and are filled with this good life that eludes us. As we humbly depend on Him and do not lean on our own understanding or strength, He guides us into His fullness that is free from strain, encumbrances and self-effort. He carries and cares for our every burden.

Psalm 42:8 (MSG)

"God promises to love me all day,
sing songs all through the night!
My life is God's prayer."

We can savor every moment of this good life with Him and in Him. Like any good father, this is His deepest desire for His children. He desires us to have a good life that is full of life. We are His pride and joy.

We do not need to work to please Him. God is already pleased and we have His favor. We need to come before Him with the heart, "What's next, Papa?" and let Him fill our lives.

Paul says in Romans 8:15 (MSG), "This resurrection life you received from God is not a timid, grave-tending life. It's adventurously expectant, greeting God with a childlike "What's next, Papa?" God's Spirit touches our spirits and confirms who we really are. We know who He is, and we know who we are: Father and children."

God will lead us into fullness of life. He designed us in our mother's womb for such a time as this. He has a purpose and a plan for our lives that is good. There is a place carved out for us that only we can fill with the unique gifts, personality and wiring that He gave us.

He desires not only for us to fill some gap in the world but for us to be filled. He desires for us to truly experience this life and His goodness all around us. Life is meant to be an adventure with Him. Not a burden or a drudgery. We are intended to go from glory to glory. We are to taste and see that the Lord is good.

I am not speaking of a rosy and unrealistic picture of life. Sometimes we can think that having a comfortable life where we are appeased is the good life. If you look at the multitude of empty and unfulfilled celebrities, being catered to and having everything you want does not fill us and give us life. This is not the kind of life I am speaking of. Being indulged and catered to brings death to our spirits and souls instead of life.

We lean not on our own understanding for what will bring us life. Instead, we acknowledge and look to Him in everything. As we look to Him as a humble, trusting child, He will guide us into a full life.

How a full life looks is different for everyone. Everyone has their own callings, passions and purposes. The way we are wired and our gifts make us unique. God will use our specific gifts, personality, and passions to lead us into places of life that He calls us into.

For Solomon, he was called to be a wise and faithful king, serving the Lord rather than serving himself like the kings around him. His purpose was to demonstrate that true wisdom is found only in God, following Him with his whole heart in the way he led the people. Solomon stood out so much in this that the Queen of Sheba came to see with her own eyes. However, Solomon failed to live the example of taking only one wife and not laying huge burdens on the people.

For Jonathan, it was being a support and encouragement to David rather than taking the place of king for himself. He denied himself the title that he was privileged to as Saul's son and followed his heart. He saw the purposes and plans of God before him and walked into them with courage and faith, although they looked different than other people would choose.

For Jeremiah, this full life came in a place of not getting married or joining in community events like others around him. It was in a place that all those in his own family betrayed him and wanted to see him dead. But he remained faithful and spoke God's words to all who would listen. Living out his calling, he shared God's heart and purposes in deep ways that most never experience.

For Peter, it was giving up his family business which he was trained and expected to go into to follow Jesus. He stepped outside of the safety and comfort of all he knew and his routines. Setting it down, leaving behind friends and beloved family, Peter stepped out to follow Jesus and learn from Him. Through following Jesus, he learned a radically different way of living life that was filled with persecution and threats of death, standing even though he was afraid. He was beaten and whipped at times. Yet he was fully alive. He followed this path faithfully, living fully, all the way to his eventual death.

Choosing God's path is not the easy path of following along with the crowd. It is not the popular path that we journey on to gain our own fame or fortune but the path that will most glorify God with our lives. It may be filled with difficulty as we pick up our cross and deny ourselves, sacrificing ourselves so that others may experience His love.

In following it, we do not gain control and become better at managing our own lives. It leads to greater dependency and surrender as we open our hands wide and hold loosely to all the world holds dearly. We willingly say yes in our heart to follow when we don't know where we are being led.

With Abraham, God called him to leave behind family, friends and all he knew in Ur. He took his wife and his nephew Lot and set out for a land he knew nothing about. All he knew was that God called him to follow this path and, like a trusting child, he obeyed and went. He remembered he was a sojourner in this world and his greatest joy was his comradeship with God.

Hebrews 11:8 (VOICE) states that: "By faith Abraham heard God's call to travel to a place he would one day receive as an inheritance; and he obeyed, not knowing where God's call would take him."

In following God's path, we will feel most alive and near to God. Like with Abraham heading to Canaan, it is not the destination of getting somewhere but the path of walking with God that forms and shapes us into who God is calling us to be.

Hebrews 11:9-10 (VOICE) goes on to say, "By faith he journeyed to the land of the promise as a foreigner; he lived in tents, as did Isaac and Jacob, his fellow heirs to the promise because Abraham looked ahead to a city with foundations, a city laid out and built by God."

Abraham did not set out to establish himself, but to follow God. It was not obtaining some end that was important, but following God where He would lead. God is our exceedingly great reward and inheritance. He is the gift, treasure, and what our souls deeply long for. He fills us and gives us life.

In following this path, we will have difficulty. Following God's path does not mean life will be easy and unburdened. Like Abraham who experienced famine and feared death at the hands of foreign leaders, we will have troubles and suffering in this life. But take courage, Jesus has overcome the world!

In difficulties and trials, we are made to be overcomers in Him. Looking to Him and trusting in childlike faith, He will carry us through every difficulty. As we look to Him and lean on Him, we will be given the strength to press on in surrendering all else.

We will learn where to place our feet. This is a step by step process. We learn to follow Him moment to moment, truth by truth in each decision we make. As we deny ourselves, we grow in our capacity to further deny ourselves and pick up our cross. In trusting Him and making the little decision in the moment, the larger decisions when they come are easier to follow.

As we place our feet in His footprints and follow Him, we become more and more like Him. We will shine with the brightness of His glory and be lights to others on how to find the hidden manna. In following His will, we will sense God's pleasure and have a contentment that most never experience.

"But friends, that's exactly who we are: children of God. And that's only the beginning. Who knows how we'll end up! What we know is that when Christ is openly revealed, we'll see him—and in seeing him, become like him" (1 John 3:2, MSG).

Lord, help us to plant our feet in Your love. Direct our path into the fullness of Your life. Give us childlike hearts that trust and follow You.

Come Out to Play!

A little prayer from my ten-year-old—

"Dear God,
I am lucky to be your son and I want to be in your life.
And when I face the night,
I know you will take care of me.
And even if something stops me,
I still will follow the path to the cross.
And even if I am not with you, I still love you, God.
If I get hurt, I know you will heal me.
If we were in a war, we would fight our enemies together.
And if I didn't have friends, I know you would help me.
And when I come to heaven,
I will come and sit next to you.
And one day I hope the world will change."
—*Thomas*

Sitting down with a sheet of paper, his imagination ran wild. Colors flung across the paper. The pen seemed to dance in his hand. Curls and swirls everywhere. The page began to take on a life of its own with animals and monsters. As he drew, he hummed one of his favorite songs. I began to sing along as I watched him work. When he was close to being done, he filled the corner of the page with hearts. He then wrote "for mom" among the hearts, smiled and handed me his work of art.

So many gifts in this child. He is a wide-eyed in wonder, bursting with energy and imagination. He makes up games to play with his friends and invites them to join in. Every day seems to be filled with new joys. He is quick to trust others, believing the best of others and quickly following along with what he is told.

In Matthew 18:3-4 (NIV), Jesus calls a little child over and says to his disciples, "'Truly I tell you,' He said, 'unless you change and become like little children, you will never enter the kingdom of heaven. Therefore, whoever humbles himself like this little child is the greatest in the kingdom of heaven.'"

The word *become* here is Strong's #1096, the Greek word *ginomai*. It means to come into being, being born, emerging or showing oneself. [1] In this way, it is a condition or a state that shows itself rather than an effort or something we strive after.

We do not need to try to be little children. When we are born again to new life, we are also being born again to a state of childlike wonder, belief and faith. God is making us more and more like little children.

Hmmm. What if God is like a father handing his child a blank sheet of paper and some colors? Our hearts to fling those colors across the page everywhere as we let our imagination run wild. A song filling up in our hearts, we can't help but hum as we work. And hearts everywhere on our pages, filling all the empty corners with love for God and those around us.

Are we willing to come out and play?

Children are present to the moment. They are not worried about the future or drudging over the past. They are alive to the present and what they are doing right now. They are filled with joy and drink in life like a sponge. They take it all in like a deep breath. Below is a poem written by a young lady, 10 years old, in Indonesia:

Rolling waves on the beach
Sounded in my ears
How beautiful God's creation
nothing else like it
—*Herpina*

In their natural state, children know how to play. They breathe in life. And then as they exhale, creativity, play and joy spill forth. They love to play and are not afraid to learn something new. They have learned to trustingly rely on their caregivers and anticipate their needs will be met. They depend upon their caregivers and have learned that they know what is best for them. And in their sweet innocence, they are filled with warmth for those close.

Children have a natural ability to be present to life and to those around them. They are great teachers of how to live more present to the moment. They teach us how to play, love and be with each other. They innocently and sweetly are present to love and life.

These are a few poems I wrote, enjoying my own children:

The Present

Present moments like sand,
sifting through my fingers
They can't be grasped or held to
Such joy
In this together song
Present to life, to You, to them
I surrender to the now
As gentle love
full of peace
surrounds us,
transforms us.
Your mother heart
Meets with mine
and brings life
that satisfies my soul

Treasure Chest

Full of joy
found in You
As I stand barefoot
On this holy ground
letting the sand
sink between my toes
Feeling the warmth of the sun
The fullness of care
You satisfy my every desire.
Standing hand in hand,
with little fingers wrapped around mine.
Our eyes brim with the fullness of our hearts
Of this together song.

Romans 8:16-17 (MSG) says, "We know who He is, and we know who we are: Father and children. And we know we are going to get what's coming to us—an unbelievable inheritance! We go through exactly what Christ goes through. If we go through the hard times with Him then we're certainly going to go through the good times with Him!"

If we do not have this Father and child image deeply imbedded, we can end up following a set of rules laid out in the Bible. We will see faith as something we do rather than something we are—loved children of God. We will work hard at following the rules and be critical of ourselves and others where we can't seem to get it right. We will try to be a good Christian by what we do rather than by who we are.

Years ago, when I was a new Christian, I was excited about everything I was learning about God. But, somewhere in my heart, I had this picture of God as distant and outside of our world, looking down from above and disapproving of all our sin.

Then one day, as I was spending time with Him in my prayer room, He gave me a vision that changed the way I saw Him. In this vision, I saw the earth, the universe, sun, stars, babies, colors, and even the grass; At that moment, I knew that He created everything and was actively aware and involved on every level with His creation—from every blade of grass that springs up to every baby that is born.

I began to have a revelation of His incredible magnitude. I understood that He stands outside of time. I saw what seemed to be an infinite amount of people from time beginning to time ending. He created each one and knew everything about them all.

Then I suddenly realized how small and insignificant I am compared to the universe and the magnitude of people. I felt so disheartened, and with tears in my eyes I asked Him, "God, where do I belong? Why would you even bother with me? I am not even a speck of dust in a moment of time."

I felt Him clearly speak to me, "Daughter, you belong at the center of my heart." At that moment, He became my Father and I knew I belonged to Him. I knew, even though I am insignificant in proportion to the universe, I am significant to Him.

That is His place for all of us, at the center of His heart. If we really understood how much we mattered to God, we would trust and depend upon Him. He is the good Father who is all wise and all knowing. He knows everything about us and loves us unconditionally. There is nothing that can change His love for us and His desire for our best.

If we deep down believe that God's love is conditional on our performance, we will love others the same way. We may hear that God loves us but believe in our heart it's conditional on our performance. What happens is that we treat our neighbor out of the paradigm of how we see God.

We may say we love our neighbor unconditionally but then avoid them as soon as they offend us. We hold them at arm's length. Then we blame our judgement on them for their behaviors. We think to ourselves, "If only they treated me differently, we would get along. They make it difficult to be around them." We do not enjoy or delight in them. We categorize people and judge them by the standards we set. These are the same standards that deep down we believe God holds us to and we measure ourselves by.

We end up living by the rules rather than out of being loved unconditionally. When we are living by the rules, even our good efforts will be off-key. When we get it right, we are stricken with self-righteousness. We end up having an air of arrogance about us. And when we fail to live up to our own expectations, we are overcome by shame and feel humiliated. Either way we lose.

Rather than flourishing in freedom, we may have a deep-seated underlying anger. When disappointments come, we try harder, work harder and end up feeling frustrated with ourselves, our faith, and others. We flounder rather than flourish. There are so many Christians that have a smile on their face but are angry underneath and they do not know why.

When we are struggling with forgiving or loving, we don't need to work harder at it, grit our teeth and make it happen. What we need is to sit in the love of God and let His heart change our heart for the person. Filled with His love for us, even in our weaknesses and shortcomings, we will be set free to love others unconditionally.

I once was really struggling with forgiveness of someone who hurt me deeply. I was wrestling in my heart about it and went into my prayer room to pray and wrestle with God over it. I felt all tangled up inside and resentment towards the other person was creeping up everywhere.

As I spent some time praying, I became frustrated and was about to leave; then a song came across the radio. It said, "Surely she has been forgiven much, she will love much." At that moment, my heart broke. All my arguments about how I was right and they were wrong fell to the ground. It was in the love of God that I could abandon my anger.

I remembered how much I had been given and forgiven by God and was able to let go of my anger and resentment. I didn't deserve His forgiveness. In receiving His unconditional love for me, I had freedom to forgive myself.

I was remembering that I came to the Lord later in life (in my 30's). I had been an alcoholic when I was a teenager. I went through years of AA and stopped drinking but had not found Jesus at that time so I was still empty and full of pain inside.

As I became older and had some years of sobriety, I went from trying to get filled by drinking to joining the workforce and trying to get filled by work. I quickly became a workaholic. Yet nothing seemed to fill all the emptiness and pain inside.

Eventually I burned out, became severely depressed, full of anxiety and almost totally incapacitated. I was terrified at what was happening to me. It was then that Jesus came in my life. Shortly after becoming a Christian, He healed me of my depression. It was like someone came in and turned the lights on.

Remembering this about myself and the forgiveness I was given by Jesus, after hearing God speak to me in the song, the next day I found myself blessing the person I had been so angry with. Gratitude and joy filled my heart for the love and forgiveness I experienced in my own life. Spending time in God's love and forgiveness for me, I found freedom to love others in their weakness and pain.

It is only in knowing this love for ourselves that we can give this love away to others. We are hard-wired to receive love and give it away to others. God created us this way.

Children, being loved by their parents naturally know how to live in love. They don't think that they must carry everything themselves. They allow others to help them. They depend on others. They receive love and give it back the same way.

As Christians, we are being born again into love. As we receive God's love, we are learning to live in trusting abandon. Adam and Eve lived this way in the garden before they sinned. They trusted and depended upon God for everything. They lived in His love naked and unashamed.

It was not eating the apple that was the first sin. It was allowing doubt of God's goodness towards them to creep in and dictate their behaviors. When doubt overtakes us, the resulting sin dictates our behavior rather than obedience in trusting abandon to His love.

We need to awaken to God's immense Fatherly love and live in it!

Living in Love

Our attitudes and perceptions impact how we handle situations and the outcome more than our circumstances. And these attitudes and perceptions are rooted in the view we hold of God. They are impacted deeply by how much of God's love we receive.

When we walk in trusting abandon, knowing God's immense love and goodness towards us, our disposition impacts our reaction. We feel loved and safe and so we are free to react in a way that reflects that our security is held in God rather than our circumstances.

Our adaptability and flexibility to solve problems effectively is rooted in this love. We have freedom when we feel loved, cherished and safe to make good decisions and adapt to unanticipated situations. When we are not living out of God's love, we will feel the need to control people and circumstances. And our ability to see rightly will be skewed by our feelings.

When we are in a place of feeling unloved and uncared for, we will most likely see things from a place of fear, confusion and accusation rather than understanding and hope. How we see depends much on our understanding how loved and cherished we are. As we are afraid, we blame and accuse ourselves, God, and others.

As an example, Job said to God in Job 10:8,11-13 (GW), "Your hands formed me and made every part of me, then you turned to destroy me... Didn't you dress me in skin and flesh and weave me together with bones and tendons? You gave me life and mercy. Your watchfulness has preserved my spirit. But in your heart you hid these things. I know this is what you did."

Job felt accused by God of sin and was caught up in negative thinking in his circumstances. He couldn't see beyond this or get himself out of it. Ever been there?

At one time, when I was feeling under a great deal of stress and pressure, I reacted to a situation in blame rather than being helpful. As soon as I realized this, I became upset at myself for my reaction. At first, my thoughts went to, "*What is wrong with me? Why can't I ever get it right? God is probably disgusted with me right now. I can't hear Him and He probably would not want to talk to me."*

Then I moved to blame my circumstances and God: "*Why do my circumstances always seem difficult? I don't have the capacity to navigate them. Why does God do this to me?*" Blame of others: "*If that person hadn't screwed up so badly or I knew earlier what help they needed, they wouldn't have put me under so much pressure.*" Fear: "*I can see all these possibilities for disaster coming from this and my quick reaction to it. It is unforgivable.*"

Blame and accusation against ourselves, God and others drains us of our vitality of life. Job was totally drained of his strength. He said in Job 6:11 (GW), "What strength that I can go on hoping? What goal do I have that I would want to prolong my life?"

For Job, he completely lost his hope and wondered why he should go on in life. In this place of hopelessness, he felt helpless and severely depressed. He proclaims in Job 6:13 (GW), "Am I not completely helpless? Haven't my skills been taken away from me?"

Job in his place of pain, confusion and feeling separated from God, deeply longed for a mediator to help Him. He speaks in Job 9:4 (GW), "There is no mediator between us to put his hand on both of us."

When he felt distant and separated from God, Job knew he needed a mediator that would help him. He needed a way to get past the issue of suffering being the result of sin and connect with God. In the story of Job, his friends could also not get past their own assumptions and judgements about sin and suffering. In Job 42:7 (VOICE), God spoke to one of the friends, Eliphaz, "My anger is burning against you and your two friends because you have not spoken rightly of Me."

The good news is God answered that prayer for a mediator when He gave us Jesus. He gave us a mediator that would act on our behalf in the face of our sin. We are not condemned for our sin, but fully forgiven. God demonstrated His deep love for us in this: "While we were still sinners, Christ died for us." (Romans 5:8, NIV).

A mediator is one who reconciles a dispute or disagreement between parties. We all fall short and need a mediator to reconcile us to God. Romans 5:10 (NIV) goes on to say, "For if, when we were enemies, we were reconciled to God by the death of his Son, much more, being reconciled, we shall be saved by his life."

1 Timothy 2:5-6 (NKJV) says, "For there is one God, and one mediator between God and men, the man Christ Jesus; Who gave himself a ransom for all, to be testified in due time."

We are never without hope or outside of God's love and forgiveness. Going back to my previous example, as I was thinking all kinds of negative thoughts and feeling distant from God, suddenly my ears tuned to the music playing in the background. It was speaking what I needed to hear: "I have not forsaken you. Neither death nor life, neither angels nor demons, neither the present nor the future, nor any powers, neither height nor depth, nor anything else in all creation will be able to separate you from My love," (from Romans 8:38).

As I received the words that were playing in the background, my perceptions and attitudes changed. I began to see differently. From feeling drained, helpless, and self-examining, I suddenly had new vigor rooted in hope. I remembered I was deeply loved and not alone in this. I had help from the One who deeply loves me and would see me through.

Hebrews 8:12 (NKJV) quotes from Exodus God speaking, "For I will be merciful to their unrighteousness and their sins and their lawless deeds I will remember no more."

What we are believing about God and His feelings towards us makes a huge difference in how we feel about ourselves and how we perceive the world around us. When we stand in the place of God's love, endless goodness and mercy towards us, we have capacity and the strength needed to navigate our situations and rise above them.

David asks the same searching question as Job did when Job asked in Job 7:17 (GW), "What is a mortal that you should make so much of him, that you should be concerned about him?" But David asked this question from the opposite position of deeply understanding God's relentless love of him. As a result, he had a totally different perspective.

David asks in Psalm 8:4-6 (GW), "What is a mortal that you remember him or the Son of Man that you take care of him? You have made him a little lower than yourself. You have crowned him with glory and honor. You have made him rule what your hands created. You have put everything under his control."

David also knew that God examined him and was very present, active and involved in his life. In Psalm 139:1-18 (HCSB), David proclaims from a position of love,

"Lord, You have searched me and known me.
You know when I sit down and when I stand up;
You understand my thoughts from far away.
You observe my travels and my rest;
You are aware of all my ways.
Before a word is on my tongue,
You know all about it, Lord.
You have encircled me;
You have placed Your hand on me.
This extraordinary knowledge is beyond me.
It is lofty; I am unable to reach it.

Where can I go to escape Your Spirit?
Where can I flee from Your presence?
If I go up to heaven, You are there;
if I make my bed in Sheol, You are there.
If I live at the eastern horizon
or settle at the western limits,
even there Your hand will lead me;
Your right hand will hold on to me.
If I say, "Surely the darkness will hide me,
and the light around me will be night"—
even the darkness is not dark to You.

The night shines like the day;
darkness and light are alike to You.
For it was You who created my inward parts;
You knit me together in my mother's womb.
I will praise You because
I have been remarkably and wonderfully made.

Your works are wonderful,
and I know this very well.
My bones were not hidden from You
when I was made in secret,
when I was formed in the depths of the earth.
Your eyes saw me when I was formless;
all my days were written in Your book and planned
before a single one of them began.

God, how difficult Your thoughts are
for me to comprehend;
how vast their sum is!
If I counted them,
they would outnumber the grains of sand;
when I wake up, I am still with You."

When we operate out of knowing that we are loved deeply by God, rather than being fearful and performance based, we see the world through eyes of expectancy, trust, hope and wonder.

We no longer feel the need to perform out of emptiness and need, but rather can give out of the freedom of what we have been given. We can love and reach out to others in overflowing joy because we have been loved so well. We don't need to fear what others will think because we know how much we are loved.

Sometimes we can know this in our head but forget it in our heart. God created us for fellowship with Him. He did not create us because He needs something from us. He does not need us to accomplish something for Him. Rather, we were created in joy, out of love, to display His glory (Romans 11:36).

Ephesians 2:10 (NASB) says that we are "God's workmanship, created in Christ Jesus to do good works, which God prepared in advance for us to do."

Workmanship is the Greek word *poiema*, Strong's #4161. The word means, 'a thing made' and translates into English as 'poem.' It indicates "a handiwork, a masterpiece." [2] We are God's poem coming to life, as we live out our lives in communion with Him doing the good works He planned for us.

When we live in the love of God and operate our lives out of this place of knowing we are deeply loved, we naturally bring God into the situations we encounter. Rather than performing, we do the 'good works' which were prepared in advance for us to do. We give away the love which has been lavished on us.

Some years ago I read about a study that was done to see how people responded when they saw someone else in need. It went something like this: They had someone drop papers all over the floor where people were busily trying to get to where they were going. Then they watched to see if people would stop and help. What was interesting is that when a person just had something good happen to them, like finding money on the floor, they were twice as likely to stop and help the person in need.

When people are freely receiving the love of God and listening to His voice which is building them up, they are going to be twice as likely to notice the person in need and stop to say something encouraging that gives them life.

Ephesians 4:29 (NCV) says, "When you talk, do not say harmful things, but say what people need—words that will help others become stronger. Then what you say will do good to those who listen to you."

We can read this verse and think it is another performance requirement. We may think that we must work hard to encourage others and help them grow stronger. While this is a good thing, in Matthew 10:8 (MSG), Jesus says to His disciples, "Give as freely as you have received!" It is out of the place of first receiving love from God that we genuinely have something to give to others.

First and foremost, when Jesus walked the earth, He was present to His Father. He never left His presence and He lived His life on the earth out of this place of receiving His Father's love and giving it away.

In John 10:30 (NIV), Jesus says, "I and the Father are one." It is standing in a position, present to God and present to others, where we possess this freedom to receive from God and then give to others.

Lord, let us ever be changing more into the image of a trusting child who lives in loving abandon. Wash away our fears, doubts, rule following, striving, and critical judgement of others and ourselves. Let us live in the abundance of Your love.

Eat What's Good for You!

To freely give as we have received, we need to come aside and receive from God. A place of receiving is the Word. Sitting in the Word restores our souls, detangles our spirit from the world, renews our mind, nourishes and refreshes us. It gives us something to be able to give out to others.

Like without any physical activity, our body languishes; Without being nourished by the Word, we languish spiritually. We become more busy, demanding and distracted.

When we are not being nourished by the Word, our focus moves more quickly away from God and onto ourselves. It's hard to identify when we are in this place but we will look for something other than God to fill us.

Often what we strive after is rooted in our expectations. We expect to have certain things in life and believe they will somehow fill us. What we labor for is not to bring glory to God but to meet first our needs and then our desires that are rooted in our expectations.

In John 6:26-27 (NIV), Jesus says to the people who were seeking Him out after He miraculously fed 5,000 people, "Very truly I tell you, you are looking for me, not because you saw the signs I performed but because you ate the loaves and had your fill. Do not work for food that spoils, but for food that endures to eternal life, which the Son of Man will give you. For on him God the Father has placed his seal of approval."

It was not that the people were hungry and needed food that Jesus was confronting. It was that they were spending their efforts laboring to be filled by something other than God. God had so much more for them in life than just food at their table.

Life is more than eating and drinking. If they would just step aside with Him long enough to see His path, they could have so much more beyond their next meal. They would find a new path filled with life, adventure and hope.

Often, even when we are looking to Jesus, we like to control our path and insist on leading the way rather than being open to the adventure He may have for us. Being in control feels safe and comfortable.

Because of this, we can sometimes presume Jesus will meet our needs or desires in some specific way. We expect Him to act according to our desires rather than being open to follow His plan. Having it our way becomes an idol and, like the Israelites being freed from Egypt, we may even grumble and complain when He does not give us what we want the way we want it.

At the time of Jesus, many of the Jewish people expected the Messiah to free them from the Romans and give them the power. In its place, Jesus offered them the living bread from heaven. Jesus offered them eternal life and a life on this earth of self-sacrifice. Instead of freeing the Jewish people from Roman rule, He told them that when the Roman soldiers asked them to carry something one mile, to carry it two.

These people became offended with Jesus for not giving them what they expected. They refused to follow Him and believe in Him because He was not going to give them the status and power they desired. In Matthew 11:6 (NASB), Jesus says, "blessed is he who does not take offense at Me."

Jesus offered instead what the people really needed instead. Deep down, what we all need, what we thirst and hunger for, is God. We were made for Him. He is the only bread that satisfies our hunger. Yet we often spend our energies day after day on bread that perishes. We labor for what we desire outside of God and have very little left over at the end of the day to offer Him.

In John 6:35 (NIV), Jesus said, "I am the bread of life. Whoever comes to me will never go hungry, and whoever believes in me will never be thirsty."

We are freely given this bread of life that will fill and satisfy us, but instead we still look around for the world to fill us. We think, if we just had more or this or that, we would be satisfied. Then when we have it, we only crave more.

Like the Israelites wandering in the wilderness, we constantly crave what we do not have. We fantasize about life with unrealistic expectations and look back and complain about what we had, and didn't appreciate at the time, and no longer have anymore.

Yet this manna that falls from the heavens is all we need. It is the sustenance that gives us life for today. Jesus is this very Word of God that nourishes us. John 1:1 (AMP) says, "In the beginning [before all-time] was the Word [Christ], and the Word was with God, and the Word was God Himself."

Jesus says in John 6:48-51 (AMP), "I am the Bread of Life [that gives and sustains life]. Your fathers ate the manna in the wilderness, and [yet] they died. [But] this is the Bread that comes down from heaven. If anyone eats of this Bread, he will live forever; and also the Bread that I shall give for the life of the world is My flesh (body)."

For forty years, the Israelites ate manna that supernaturally came down every day from heaven. Exodus 16:4 (NIV) says, "Then the Lord said to Moses, 'I will rain down bread from heaven for you. The people are to go out each day and gather enough for that day. In this way I will test them and see whether they will follow my instructions.'"

Manna was the sustenance that the people of God lived on. It was freely provided. It was a bread-like substance they would cook up with oil. If you tried to store it up, it would rot. You were provided enough for the day so you needed to come back the next day for more.

It represented God's provision and nourishment. Nehemiah 9:15 (NIV) says, "In their hunger You gave them bread from heaven and in their thirst You brought them water from the rock; You told them to go in and take possession of the land You had sworn with uplifted hand to give them."

Manna was a type and shadow of the real bread from heaven—Jesus. He is our daily nourishment. John 6:31-35 (AMP) says, "Our forefathers ate the manna in the wilderness; as the Scripture says, 'He gave them bread out of heaven to eat.'"

Jesus then said to them, "I assure you, most solemnly I tell you, Moses did not give you the Bread from heaven [what Moses gave you was not the Bread from heaven], but it is My Father Who gives you the true heavenly Bread.

For the Bread of God is He Who comes down out of heaven and gives life to the world. Then they said to Him, 'Lord, give us this bread always (all the time)!' Jesus replied, 'I am the Bread of Life. He who comes to Me will never be hungry, and he who believes in and cleaves to and trusts in and relies on Me will never thirst any more (at any time).'"

Too often, we labor for the bread that does not truly nourish us rather than that which fills and satisfies. We seek to fill ourselves with what we can reach and touch rather than what is eternal and will bring genuine life. As we try to fill ourselves with something else to satisfy us, it leaves us empty inside. Life seems to elude us and be just out of our reach.

We reach and strive after the bread that fails to nourish us and we languish inside. And as we strive after what does not fill us, we don't take the time to be nourished by the Word of God. We become too busy to sit down, read the Word and let God speak to us. We then increasingly labor and strive in vain for that which can never satisfy us. It is only as we look to God and His Word that we will be genuinely nourished and filled.

We become more like our teacher when we let our mind and heart be transformed by the Word of God. We don't naturally think like God. In Isaiah 55:8-9 (NIV), the Lord says, "For My thoughts are not your thoughts, neither are your ways My ways... As the heavens are higher than the earth, so are My ways higher than your ways and My thoughts than your thoughts."

Rather, we need to have our mind renewed. Paul says in Romans 12:2 (NKJV), "And do not be conformed to this world, but be transformed by the renewing of your mind, that you may prove what is that good and acceptable and perfect will of God."

We let the light in and renew our minds through the Word of God. We replace our thought patterns and attitudes with His. Opening our hearts and minds to the Word of God transforms us from the inside out.

Psalm 19:8 (NIV) says, "The precepts of the Lord are right, giving joy to the heart. The commands of the Lord are radiant, giving light to the eyes."

Jesus was passionate about the Word of God when He walked on the earth. He used it in everything He said and did. When He was led into the wilderness and tested, He used the Word of God to fight off attacks from Satan. Right after His time of testing in the wilderness, He went into the synagogue on the Sabbath, as was the custom, and read a passage (Luke 4:16).

He read, "The Spirit of the LORD is upon Me, because He has anointed Me to preach the gospel to the poor; He has sent Me to heal the brokenhearted, to proclaim liberty to the captives and recovery of sight to the blind, to set at liberty those who are oppressed; To proclaim the acceptable year of the Lord" (Luke 4:18-19, NKJV). He sat down and then said, "Today this Scripture is fulfilled in your hearing" (Luke 4:21, NKJV).

It was the Word of God that proclaimed and probably revealed to Jesus His ministry purpose. The Word was alive to Jesus, just as it is available for each one of us today.

The best way to read the Bible is with an open heart of humility, curiosity and willingness to learn as a child. Rather than reading from our intellect for knowledge, we read from our hearts, in wonder and awe as we marvel at who God is and what He might have for us.

As a child expects their parents to care for them and speak to them, we come before Him anticipating Him to speak to us. We know He is the source of knowledge that will guide our path wisely. We do not need to figure out all the answers or have everything laid before us. Receiving our "manna" and knowing the step for today is all we need. We allow the Scripture to nurse us as milk and meat for all we need to accomplish that day.

If we are bored by what we are reading in Scripture, our hearts are not connecting to it. Putting ourselves into position to receive His love and sit in His presence can sometimes help us re-connect with His Word in a meaningful way.

Other times, it may be that our lives are so cluttered and full of distractions that we just cannot focus. We look at the Word and quickly look away to social media or other distraction that keeps us from having the time to meaningfully engage with God. We do not take time to listen and reflect so we fail to really hear what God may speak to us.

Or, at times we might just need another way to connect with God that is different than the past. Sometimes changing the practice we are using in reading the Word or using a different translation of the Bible can help us to reconnect from the heart. I frequently switch translations as I read the Bible. Reading it in a different version helps me to see it from a slightly different perspective each time and keep me actively engaged.

Reading the Word is opening ourselves up to be nourished and fed by God. As we open our hearts for Him to speak to us, coming as a child, we are inviting Him to love on us. In this place, He speaks, guides, and directs us.

James 1:5 (NIV) says, "If any of you lacks wisdom, you should ask God, who gives generously to all without finding fault, and it will be given to you."

The Word is referred to by Paul in 1 Corinthians 3:2 as the sustenance that nourishes us spiritually. Like milk and meat, it satisfies the needs of the body of Christ. We ingest it, digest it and it gives us what is vital to function as the body of Christ and bear fruit.

We not only need to read the Word, but let it work in us. It is the digestive process that helps us to put it into practice, letting it work in our heart and mind. Hebrews 4:12 (NIV) says, "For the Word of God is living and active. Sharper than any double-edged sword, it penetrates even to dividing soul and spirit, joints and marrow; it judges the thoughts and attitudes of the heart."

Jesus says in Luke 8:21 (NIV), "My mother and brothers are those who hear God's Word and put it into practice." It is not in legalistically trying to fulfill the law by our own self-effort that we are transformed. This just makes us rigid and self-righteous. It is by letting the light in, shaping our hearts, thoughts and attitudes—which then changes our behaviors from the inside out.

Jesus notes in the parable of the sower (Luke 8:11-15), three ways in which the Word of God can be choked out, not creating transformation. One way is that it is stolen in unbelief. Another way is it doesn't take root and is choked out by testing. The third way is when it is choked out by life's worries, riches and pleasures. It is only when it is heard with belief and trust that it genuinely takes root and then bears fruit.

When the Word takes root, it will always bear good fruit in our lives. Luke 8:15 (NIV) says, "But the seed on good soil stands for those with a noble and good heart, who hear the Word, retain it, and by persevering produce a crop."

When we are full of worries about life, or seeking to be filled by the riches or pleasures of the world, the Word of God does not take root in our heart. Worry, indulgence and self-seeking clutter up our heart and, like weeds springing up, choke-out the Word.

After Jesus performed the miracle of feeding the people with five barely loaves and two small fish, where Jesus told them in John 6:27 (AMP),

> "Stop toiling and doing and producing for the food that perishes and decomposes [in the using], but strive and work and produce rather for the [lasting] food which endures [continually] unto life eternal; the Son of Man will give (furnish) you that, for God the Father has authorized and certified Him and put His seal of endorsement upon Him."

They went on to ask Him in John 6:28-30 (AMP), "'What are we to do, that we may [habitually] be working the works of God? [What are we to do to carry out what God requires?]'

Jesus replied, 'This is the work (service) that God asks of you: that you believe in the One Whom He has sent [that you cleave to, trust, rely on, and have faith in His Messenger].'"

The works that God is looking for us to perform are not works of hard labor but faith and belief in Jesus. It is not by our own strength that we do the works of God but in His strength and power. Often, we need to come to an end of ourselves to learn to let go of our ways. It is learning to trust as a child and enter the adventure with God.

When we are doing the works that God is looking for—looking to Him and believing in Him—He can nourish us, filling and satisfying our deepest needs. When we work hard to try to please Him in our own strength, we become exhausted and depleted.

In performing to earn His approval or working to try to please Him, it is not our belief that is at work but our lack of belief. Some of the deepest internal struggles we have in this are rooted in an inability to believe that He will love us at our worst. Coming from a performance-oriented society, we can have a hard time believing when we are not performing well that He will still care for us the same.

Psalm 127:1-2 (AMP) says, "Except the Lord builds the house, they labor in vain who build it; except the Lord keeps the city, the watchman wakes but in vain. It is vain for you to rise up early, to take rest late, to eat the bread of [anxious] toil—for He gives [blessings] to His beloved in sleep."

God is continually loving towards us and lavishly pouring out His blessings upon us. Our job is not to work to feel deserving of His blessings but to receive His love and believe in His care for us. It is learning to rest and be nourished by His love.

David knew a place of rest in the arms of God that was truly nourishing to his soul. David cries out in Psalm 131:1-3 (NIV), "Lord, my heart is not haughty, nor my eyes lofty; neither do I exercise myself in matters too great or in things too wonderful for me. Surely I have calmed and quieted my soul; like a weaned child with his mother, like a weaned child is my soul within me [ceased from fretting]. O Israel, hope in the Lord from this time forth and forever."

Can we come to a place of rest in His arms? It is in rest and knowing deeply that we are loved that we enter the flow of being led by His Spirit.

He invites us into an adventure of the unknown that is walking hand and hand with Him, putting our hands to what our hearts prompt. Entering this flow of trust and rest, we come fully alive. We step into new places with Him, knowing He will sustain us.

Sometimes instead, we stand on the sidelines with our arms crossed doubting His goodness for us. How this looks for me is rather than resting in a place where I am nourished continually by God, I work at my relationship with Him. I feel guilty when I am not doing anything. And when I am at my worst, I feel He sees me as unlovable.

When I am in a performance mentality, I am operating out of an underlying belief that in some way, I need to 'earn my keep.' I think in terms of being deserving rather than resting in His love in gratitude. When I perform well, I feel deserving of His love. However, when I feel deserving or entitled, I cannot also be grateful.

We can struggle sometimes to believe we are loved and can do nothing to earn God's approval. It is tough work to allow ourselves to be loved unconditionally even when we are at our worst. But the truth is He loves us, cares for us, will be there for us and will provide for us no matter what.

When we are in performance mode, we can feel entitled to the blessings He bestows. We think we earned them and the blessings are our just rewards. And if they are taken away, like Jonah who was angry with God about taking away a plant that was giving him shade, we feel angry about it like it is an injustice done to us.

And when we don't get it right, we feel shame. There is a little voice that tells us there is something wrong with us for not performing. We feel like a loser. For me, old tapes of rejection play in my head.

So, to prove this little voice wrong, we may grit our teeth and try harder to get it right. In gritting our teeth and white knuckling it, we do the right thing out of a disordered place rather than a place of solid security from being loved. We are trying to get it right so that we can be loved and accepted rather than doing the right thing out of a place of being filled to overflowing.

Performance gets us to a place of focusing on ourselves and our own behaviors rather than on God. When we get it right, we feel self-righteous and when we don't, we feel shame.

The other direction we can go with self-effort is to give up. We tell ourselves it doesn't matter and so we don't try. We are riddled with overwhelming self-doubt and wonder why we can never seem to get past it. It holds us down and back as it is all about us, our gifts, our abilities and our deficiencies.

Or, out of frustration, we act out in the other direction. We might tell ourselves, *"if I can't be good, then I might as well be bad."* We give in to what the heck responses. We think, *"I already blew it so what the heck, I might as well just give in and indulge myself."* Instead of trying to do good, we do the opposite.

My littlest son sometimes has struggled with this. He has gone in the wrong direction because he was frustrated. He had an incredibly tough start to life with no breaks before he came into my life. Everything was hard for him because he just wasn't given the opportunity to develop his motor skills or abilities. Seeing kids doing more than him frustrated him and made him angry with himself. In those places of deep frustration, he would act out his anger at times.

I think to myself, if he just knew how much God loved Him and was pleased with him. If he just knew how much I love him and am pleased with him, not for anything he does or gets right but for who he is—my beloved son; God's beloved son.

Receiving God's love and acceptance that we already have gets us to a relaxed state of being ourselves. We enter in the unforced rhythms of grace.

The works of God are not self-created works. They do not depend upon us getting everything right. They are not hindered by our flaws or inadequacies. They are not based upon us, our abilities, or our limitations. The works of God are from God and bring Him glory.

As an example, Moses stuttered. So, when God called him to go back to Egypt and tell the Pharaoh to let his people go, swimming in self-doubt, he looked at his abilities and told God to send someone else instead. Like most of us, he just couldn't get past his self-doubt and inadequacies.

But God was trying to get him to see that the kingdom works are not based in his abilities but in God's abilities. The works of God are kingdom works with God at the center rather than ourselves at the center. They bring God glory.

Moses finally said yes and stepped into the adventure with God. It led him back to Egypt to free the Israelites from bondage. Entering the adventure with God and depending upon Him, Moses saw plagues poured out from heaven and God supernaturally setting His people free. He saw the ocean split before him, a cloud of glory lead him and fire follow behind him for protection.

He had finally realized that he, and all the people of God, were radically loved by God. God was providing for all that they needed. Life was a journey that had meaning because God went with them on it.

When Moses finally brought the people of God to the Promised Land, he peered over into the land but never entered it. The Promised Land was not a destination, it was what Moses found along the pathway of following God's will. It was the daily manna from heaven of God's love and care that nourished him. It was the adventure of saying yes, despite his fears, weaknesses and inadequacies. This was the true Promised Land.

If Moses had traveled the whole journey just to enter the Promised Land, he would have been bitter to find that he did it all for nothing and never received the promise himself. The journey was not for nothing, the journey itself with God was everything.

Sometimes what we are working for is solely to satisfy our own needs and desires and we don't even see it. Our focus is on ourselves rather than His kingdom. What we are hoping from Jesus is not for His kingdom to come and having the opportunity to sacrifice in being part of bringing it forth, but, like in John 6:26-27, for Him to perform some miracle to meet our immediate needs.

In John 4:31-34 (AMP), the disciples urged Jesus to eat something. He responded, "I have food (nourishment) to eat of which you know nothing and have no idea. So the disciples said one to another, has someone brought Him something to eat? Jesus said to them, My food (nourishment) is to do the will (pleasure) of Him Who sent Me and to accomplish and completely finish His work."

His work was His belief and His nourishment came in doing God's will out of a place of belief. In John 6:30 (AMP), the people said to Jesus, "What sign (miracle, wonderwork) will You perform then, so that we may see it and believe and rely on and adhere to You? What [supernatural] work have You [to show what You can do]?"

They were looking for Him to meet their immediate needs for bread. They went on to tell Him in John 6:11 (AMP), "Our forefathers ate the manna in the wilderness; as the Scripture says, He gave them bread out of heaven to eat."

Jesus didn't scorn them for coming to Him with their immediate needs in asking for a sign to help their belief. Rather He turned them to look not only to their physical needs, but to Himself, who satisfies every need. He responded in John 6:35 (AMP), "I am the Bread of Life. He who comes to me will never be hungry, and he who believes in and cleaves to and trusts in and relies on Me will never thirst any more (at any time)."

There were also times Jesus was angry when the Israelites asked for a sign. He became angry when the religious leaders were looking for Jesus to prove His authority to them. They were not coming to Jesus humbly in need and lack of belief asking for Him to meet them there. But, they came to Him in self-righteousness demanding Him to justify Himself in their unbelief.

Matthew 12:38-39 (AMP) says,

> "Then some of the scribes and Pharisees said to Him, Teacher, we desire to see a sign or miracle from You [proving that You are what You claim to be]. But He replied to them, an evil and adulterous generation (a generation morally unfaithful to God) seeks and demands a sign; but no sign shall be given to it except the sign of the prophet Jonah."

Jesus wants us to look to Him to meet our needs. David proclaims in Psalm 103:2-6 (AMP),

> "Bless (affectionately, gratefully praise) the Lord, O my soul, and forget not [one of] all His benefits—
>
> Who forgives [every one of] all your iniquities, Who heals [each one of] all your diseases, Who redeems your life from the pit and corruption, Who beautifies, dignifies, and crowns you with loving-kindness and tender mercy;
>
> Who satisfies your mouth [your necessity and desire at your personal age and situation] with good so that your youth, renewed, is like the eagle's [strong, overcoming, soaring]! The Lord executes righteousness

> and justice [not for me only, but] for all who
> are oppressed."

Ultimately, in receiving what we need from Jesus, we come to a place of trusting Him, knowing He is more than enough to meet our every need. As we learn to trust in His love for us and are daily nourished by His love, we become free to serve Him with our eyes on His kingdom purposes.

Even when life is difficult and we are performing poorly, we can trust that He will meet us there. He will not leave us and forsake us. If we let Him, He will soothe all our doubts and calm our fears. He will remind us how loved we are and how much we matter to Him.

When life was difficult and I was performing poorly, I used to struggle with a fear of disaster. When I was in an adversarial situation, rather than trusting in God's care and defense of me, I would think it was my responsibility to get it right and perform well so God would approve of me. I put all the pressure on myself rather than resting in His care and provision for me.

David was someone that knew that even when he blew it while he was facing difficulty and adversaries, that God would care for him. He could look to God who would never forsake him. God would deliver David out of his trouble in His goodness and lovingkindness.

David cries out in Psalm 127:9-14 (AMP),

> "Hide not Your face from me; turn not Your
> servant away in anger, You Who have been

> my help! Cast me not off, neither forsake me, O God of my salvation! Although my father and my mother have forsaken me, yet the Lord will take me up [adopt me as His child] ...
>
> Give me not up to the will of my adversaries, for false witnesses have risen up against me; they breathe out cruelty and violence. [What, what would have become of me] had I not believed that I would see the Lord's goodness in the land of the living! Wait and hope for and expect the Lord; be brave and of good courage and let your heart be stout and enduring. Yes, wait and hope for and expect the Lord."

We need not fear disaster when the enemy rises up against us because the Lord has promised to deliver us in the day of trouble.

Psalm 91:14-15 (AMP) says,

> "Because he has set his love upon Me, therefore will I deliver him; I will set him on high, because he knows and understands My name [has a personal knowledge of My mercy, love, and kindness—trusts and relies on Me, knowing I will never forsake him, no, never]. He shall call upon Me, and I will answer him; I will be with

> him in trouble, I will deliver him and honor him."

It is in a place of lack of belief in God taking care of all our needs and lack of nourishment from His love that we seek to fill our needs by other means. We strive because we are not receiving God's love. We have a deep inner need to be loved. If we are not filled by God's love, we will naturally seek to fill this emptiness by something else.

And sometimes the clutter in our lives from having so much abundance can cause us to become more and more empty. As our lives are filled with more and more stuff, we may find ourselves distracted and drawn away from the God who once was so near.

In Deuteronomy 6:10-15 (AMP), Moses warns the people,

> "And when the Lord your God brings you into the land which He swore to your fathers, to Abraham, Isaac, and Jacob, to give you, with great and goodly cities which you did not build, and houses full of all good things which you did not fill, and cisterns hewn out which you did not hew, and vineyards and olive trees which you did not plant, and when you eat and are full, then beware lest you forget the Lord, Who brought you out of the land of Egypt, out of the house of bondage.
>
> You shall [reverently] fear the Lord your God and serve Him and swear by His name

> [and presence]. You shall not go after other gods, any of the gods of the peoples who are round about you; For the Lord your God in the midst of you is a jealous God; lest the anger of the Lord your God be kindled against you, and He destroy you from the face of the earth."

When we are being nourished and filled by God, we will be able to give out of our abundance to all those around us in need. Psalm 37:26 (NIV) says about the righteous, "They are always generous and lend freely; their children will be blessed."

When we are not being nourished by God's love, we are constantly looking for that which will nourish us. This was the case of the leaders of Israel. Instead of being a fountain of nourishment to others whom they were sent to care for, they were looking for what they could get from the Israelites. They were seeking to be served rather than serving.

The Lord says in Ezekiel 34:2-4 (AMP),

> "Woe to the [spiritual] shepherds of Israel who feed themselves! Should not the shepherds feed the sheep? You eat the fat, you clothe yourselves with the wool, you kill the fatlings, but you do not feed the sheep.

> The diseased and weak you have not strengthened, the sick you have not healed, the hurt and crippled you have not bandaged, those gone astray you have not brought back, the lost you have not sought to find, but with force and hardhearted harshness you have ruled them."

It is easy to stand on the outside and see that as being wrong, but the subtlety was that the sheep were livestock. The purpose of sheep was to provide wool and food. There is a temptation to see them based upon our needs rather than their needs.

One way this can come to play is when we become critical rather than grateful and start thinking that others are not serving us well. We are not paying attention to their needs but our own. When they don't serve us well, we think that they are purposely insulting us or causing us harm.

For instance, someone can come into a coffee shop expecting to be served rather than serve. When the woman at the counter makes a mistake and forgets the cream in their coffee, instead of wondering what the server might be going through or the tough day they are already having *(which would result in seeking a way to bless them or refresh them),* the person purchasing the coffee becomes insulted and leaves in a huff without giving a tip.

This person is not thinking about tending to the needs of this server by considering how they could "wash their feet" like Jesus might have. They are ruling over them with hardhearted harshness. They are expecting the person to meet them at their expectations rather than looking for what they can generously give out of what they have for this person's benefit.

Another person could have come into the coffee shop and received coffee from someone who forgot the cream and still be incredibly grateful that they received good tasting coffee and fast service. Rather than complain and leave in a huff, they could thank the server, pray for them, and leave them a big tip.

One can also ask the question of serving or being served on their job: Are the people who report to me strengthened and healed in their areas of weakness or are they worn-down, burnt-out and feeling spent? Do I give life to others around me or take away life?

The whole reason I went into leadership was that my first boss out of college believed in me and empowered me, giving me room to grow and use my gifts. I would not be where I am today without his encouragement, mentorship and support. It made me want to become a boss and do the same for others.

However, when I am not being nurtured by God, it is easier to fall into trying to perform for approval. I forget that I am there to serve the people who report to me and start focusing on everything that needs to get done at the expense of taking the time to strengthen and heal those who report to me and need the extra care and attention.

This is a poem I wrote to God in a season where I was really struggling with performance:

I don't want to just get the answers right;
I don't want to just live for this life.
I want so much more than the world can give;
Would you teach me to really live?
Would you meet me where I am here?
There used to be so much I would fear.
I no longer struggle the same with the worry or self-doubt;
No longer suffer under the weight of it all.
More yet, my life once so filled with despair,
Joy and peace have become my fare.
What more, dear Father, could I ask of You?
Your goodness has more than seen me through.
My shoes have not worn and my needs more than met;
Yet there is more I'm longing for yet—
You are my treasure the One that I long,
That I would be nearer to this One whom I belong.
That every day would be filled with Your touch;
That my life would speak that I love You so much.
Teach me to like Jacob to say yes in it all;
Teach me like him to offer You my all.

Performance was also the struggle with the Israelites who were fasting and praying, going through the motions of all the religious activity they thought would be approved by God, in Isaiah 58. While fasting, they sought their own pleasure, drove their workers and were contentious. The Lord said that rather than oppressing others and being full of strife and debate, they were to humble themselves and serve those around them. He promised, then their light would break out like the sun, they would be healed and have all they need.

In serving others and giving our lives away, our whole countenance changes. We are lights in darkness that shine with the light of Christ.

The Lord says in Isaiah 58:9b-10 (AMP), "If you take away from your midst yokes of oppression [wherever you find them], the finger pointed in scorn [toward the oppressed or the godly], and every form of false, harsh, unjust, and wicked speaking, And if you pour out that with which you sustain your own life for the hungry and satisfy the need of the afflicted, then shall your light rise in darkness, and your obscurity and gloom become like the noonday."

Lord, forgive us when we labor for the bread that does not satisfy. Teach us to rest in Your presence and take in what You so freely provide. Thank You for Your daily nourishment in the Word of God. Thank you that You are the Bread that fills our hungering souls with that which satisfies. From this place of nourishment, make us bread broken to feed others.

Lord, make me (us) an instrument of your peace.
Where there is hatred, let me (us) sow love.
Where there is injury, pardon.
Where there is doubt, faith.
Where there is despair, hope.
Where there darkness, light.
Where there is sadness, joy.

O Divine Master,
grant that I (we) may not so much seek
to be consoled, as to console;
to be understood, as to understand;
to be loved, as to love.
For it is in giving that we receive.
It is in pardoning that we are pardoned,
and it is in dying that we are born to Eternal Life."
—Prayer of St. Francis

Shine!

Ever notice how when people lie they hide their eyes from you? They hide in the shadows and avoid the light.

John 3:20-21 (NIV) says, "Everyone who does evil hates the light, and will not come into the light for fear that their deeds will be exposed. But whoever practices the truth comes into the light, so that it may be clearly seen that what he has done has been accomplished in God."

Light, in this case is the illumination of the Spirit. We are to be the light of this world that shines brightly and illuminates the truth that the Light has come into this world. God is the Great Light and in Him there is no darkness (1 John 1:5).

So how do we live as 'children of light'? Paul says in Ephesians 5:8-11 (NIV), "For you were once in darkness, but now you are light in the Lord. Live as children of light, for the fruit of the light consists in all goodness, righteousness, and truth, and find out what pleases the Lord. Having nothing to do with the fruitless deeds of darkness, but rather expose them."

Children of light live in the light and are enlightened through the Holy Spirit who indwells them, pointing others to the True Light. The light in us bears witness that there is a greater Light among us. And in this place of living in the light, we bear fruit of the Light—goodness, righteousness, and truth.

John 12:46 (NIV) says, "I have come as a light into the world, that whoever believes in Me should not abide in darkness." The light exposes the darkness and brings conviction upon it. It can be uncomfortable as it exposes sin so that one turns away and walks toward righteousness.

Light is the Greek word *phos*. It first and foremost means the manifestation of the Spirit. Light represents God's presence. It is also an illumination of the Spirit. Light allows one to see what was dark before. It exposes openly in the view of all what was hidden. It brings conviction of sin. The Spirit of God illuminates the truth together with the spiritual purity associated with it. [3]

The light can be uncomfortable. But at the same time, it contains divine illumination that reveals and imparts the life of Christ. [3] As plants need the light to thrive, living more fully in the light causes us to grow into greater life.

Those who live in the darkness of intentional sin do not want to be exposed and live openly in the light. Often, they put on a front to be approved of and accepted by others, not even knowing their real purpose in life through God. They seek to get their needs for love and acceptance met by the world in the only ways they know how, by pretending and performing for others.

Many of the religious leaders in the time of Jesus lived this way. They pretended and performed because they valued status and approval of men. While they proclaimed to be experts in the Torah and follow God, they didn't even know Him. They used religion for their own gain.

In John 5:41-44 (NKJV), Jesus says to the religious leaders, "I do not receive honor from men. But I know you, that you do not have the love of God in you. I have come in My Father's name, and you do not receive Me; if another comes in his own name, him you will receive. How can you believe, who receive honor from one another, and do not seek the honor that comes from the only God?"

However, believing in Christ does not instantly stop people from seeking honor of men and bring people to a place of feeling comfortable about who they are in Christ. It also does not necessarily give them the willingness needed to fully live in the light.

John 12:42-43 (NKJV) says, "Nevertheless even among the rulers many believed in Him, but because of the Pharisees they did not confess Him, lest they should be put out of the synagogue; for they loved the praise of men more than the praise of God."

The good news is that Jesus does not leave us in this place if we truly put our faith in Him. He convicts us of our sin and sets us progressively free from hiding, fitting in, and people pleasing. We begin to more and more live in the light of who we were made to be, honoring God with our lives.

An example is Nicodemus. He was a Pharisee and ruler of the Jews that first came to Jesus by night. He believed and confessed that he knew Jesus was from God (John 3:2). Later, in John 7:50 (NKJV), when the Pharisees and chief priests wanted to arrest Jesus, Nicodemus spoke up and said, "Does our law judge any man before it hears him and knows what he does?"

However, it was not until after Jesus was crucified that Nicodemus was willing to come out of hiding and be seen as a follower of Christ. After Jesus died, Nicodemus accompanied Joseph, another one who was secretly a disciple for fear of the Jews. They took His body to prepare it for burial (John 19:38-39).

Hiding is something that came about with the original sin in the garden. When Adam and Eve ate of the fruit from the tree of the knowledge of good and evil, their eyes were opened to their nakedness. They quickly worked to cover themselves. Then when the Lord came back into the garden to walk with them, they hid themselves. Adam told God, "I heard Your voice in the garden, and I was afraid because I was naked; and I hid myself" (Genesis 3:6-10, NASB).

The feeling that Adam and Eve were experiencing that caused them to hide and cover up was shame. Shame is the feeling that there is something flawed about us that, if revealed and exposed, would make us unaccepted by others.

Brene Brown defines shame as "the intensely painful feeling or experience of believing that we are flawed and therefore unworthy of love and belonging." [4]

Because of feelings of shame, we hide truth about ourselves and cover it up. We are afraid that if it is exposed, people will think less of us. Just as the religious leaders in Jesus day who put on a show for everyone, we fear rejection and banishment from our community. So those feelings of shame push us to pretending, covering and hiding.

Brene Brown notes that shame is about who we are. All people experience the feeling of shame at some points along their life. She notes that when we are shamed and keep it locked up inside of us, it festers and grows. It is bringing shame out and speaking about our experiences with people we trust that shame loses its power over us and we begin to cultivate resilience. [5]

Before I came to Christ, I held a shame-based identity. I believed there was something deeply wrong with me at the core that could not be uncovered. One with a shame-based identity lives in continual hiding, believing that if we are exposed for what we think, feel, believe, and value, we will certainly be rejected.

When we live in shame, we live in fear of being exposed for who we really are. Truthfully, we don't even know who we are because we never risk exercising our beliefs and values for others to see. We hold back for risk of potentially standing out in a negative light. Instead, we go along with the crowd and try to fit in the best we can.

One who lives in a shame-based identity looks more like a chameleon, changing its colors with its environment to not be noticed or exposed—only doing and saying what is acceptable to the crowd they are in.

One way a shame-based identity develops is from being frequently shamed over long periods of time, such as when parents use this as the form of discipline growing up. Shaming is a common practice in some homes, schools, workplaces and societies to get people to conform to certain behaviors.

When I was in junior high school, I had a serious drinking problem and went through various treatment programs before I eventually became sober. Most the treatment centers I experienced were very supportive and helpful in making the changes needed in my life.

However, one of the treatment centers I went through would use shame to control people's behaviors. In this place, the one being punished was put in front of their peers wearing a sign for their behavior. This was to warn others not to do the same and to humiliate the one being shamed for their wrong choices.

While this kept many from doing any behaviors that would stand out, it did not help us to learn or grow. It created a fear and control based environment. Rather than changing, people became better at hiding and pretending.

At different points in my walk with God, He gave me freedom and delivered me from a shame-based identity. As I became increasingly delivered from this belief, it has given me freedom to become who God has made me to be.

I am more and more free to share my beliefs, values, thoughts and ideas without worrying about if they are different than what others believe. I am free to stand out, own my story and become more and more me—even in all my weaknesses.

Jesus tells the Jews who believed in Him in John 8:31 (NKJV), "If you abide in My Word, you are My disciples indeed. And you shall know the truth, and the truth shall make you free."

Shame moves us away from others and from God. We deal with it by hiding, withdrawing, or people pleasing and pretending. Or we may even have an attitude that keeps people away. The purpose of shame is to close us down. And it not only closes us down to other people but in doing so, closes us down to God.

Freedom from shame, on the other hand, opens us up to being vulnerable and authentic with others. When we are secure in the love of God just as we are, we can risk having our weaknesses exposed to others. We can risk rejection. In being vulnerable and authentic with people who are safe, we are also more open to God. And there is deep healing that happens when we are loved in our weaknesses.

Paul notes in 2 Corinthians 12:9 (NIV), "But He said to me, 'My grace is sufficient for you, for my power is made perfect in weakness.' Therefore I will boast all the more gladly about my weaknesses, so that Christ's power may rest on me."

Continually coming into the light, allowing the darkness to be exposed and washed away while becoming more authentic takes courage. We cultivate authenticity on our part by a practice of moving towards others in greater truth and vulnerability.

To live in the light means to live in the fullness of truth, genuinely and authentically. In this place of humility and vulnerability, we give glory to God.

It does not mean we need to share our greatest secrets with everyone around us. There are people who would use our vulnerability to harm us. In Matthew 7:6 (NIV) Jesus warns, "Do not give dogs what is sacred; do not throw your pearls to pigs. If you do, they may trample them under their feet, and turn and tear you to pieces."

We need those whom we can trust and be vulnerable with. As we open ourselves up to be loved by them, we heal. We can only be loved by ourselves and others to the degree we are willing to be honest and authentic about who we really are. If we genuinely want to be loved by others, we need to let others see even our weaknesses and imperfections.

Love not only sees who people are in their weaknesses with compassion but also sees the potential for who they are becoming. Paul says in 1 Corinthians 13 that love hopes all things and believes all things. And in this place of vulnerability with all our weaknesses and imperfections, along with the potential of who we are becoming, we open ourselves up to genuine humility.

Paul says in Romans 12:3 (NIV), "For by the grace given me I say to every one of you: Do not think of yourself more highly than you ought, but rather think of yourself with sober judgment, in accordance with the measure of faith God has given you."

Seeing oneself with sober judgment does not mean being overly critical of ourselves, but being real about who we are, in light of who Christ is making us to be, and our belief in His ability to complete the work that He started.

Humility is acknowledging our weaknesses in a circle of love and mercy. We admit our shortcomings in the light of also knowing how precious we are to God and the wonderful work we are and He is doing within us.

David proclaims in humility in Psalm 139:14 (NIV), "I praise you because I am fearfully and wonderfully made; Your works are wonderful, I know that full well."

When we can receive our own weaknesses in the light of God's mercy and love, we also learn to love others in this same way. We can only love others as well as we love ourselves. Humility gives us grace to love others in their imperfections and see the potential of who they can become in Christ.

Pride is about superiority. When we feel superior to others it is often because we are comparing other's weaknesses to our strengths. We are not seeing ourselves rightly. Rather, we are putting our confidence in our own strengths. Pride is not open and vulnerable or compassionate. It seeks to compare oneself and show up another.

When we have a performance mentality and judge our own worth based upon what we accomplish, pride can result. We are trusting in ourselves rather than God. Pride often feeds perfectionism as one strives for their worth by doing everything right. Then when we get it all right, we become self-righteous and proud. However, when we fail or our weaknesses are exposed so we do not look good in comparison to others, we feel insecure and inadequate.

With a performance mentality, our worth is based upon what we are doing rather than our faith in God. And when we are operating out of a performance mentality, we are drawing others to ourselves and not to God. We think to ourselves 'look how good I am' versus 'look how good God has been to me'. We are seeking equality with God by getting everything right.

Paul says in Philippians 2:5-8 (NASB) says, "Have this attitude in yourselves which was also in Christ Jesus, who, although He existed in the form of God, did not regard equality with God a thing to be grasped, but emptied Himself, taking the form of a bond-servant, and being made in the likeness of men. Being found in appearance as a man, He humbled Himself by becoming obedient to the point of death, even death on a cross."

It takes humility in our lives to connect others to God. When we are authentic, letting others in to see who we really are with all our weaknesses and imperfections, it reveals God's hand, goodness and grace in our lives. People can see God at work and are drawn to Him rather than us.

There is a sacrifice in being authentic. We risk something in being open and vulnerable and sharing of ourselves. We also are giving up an image of ourselves that we could display for other's sake. We lose something so others may gain. God is glorified.

Sharing our weaknesses and being open and vulnerable takes not only humility but sacrificial love. Love is a fruit that is born of the Spirit. As we look to the Lord and live more and more authentically, we are transformed more into His likeness and bear the fruit of His Spirit.

He shines brightly in our life and cannot be hidden. Jesus says in Luke 16:16 (NIV), "No one lights a lamp and hides it in a clay jar or puts it under a bed. Instead, they put it on a stand, so that those who come in can see the light."

Being who we are and who we are created to be exalts Christ. Jesus says in Matthew 5:15 (NIV), "In the same way, let your light shine before men, that they may see your good deeds and praise your Father in heaven."

It is in being authentic and living in the light that we bear fruit of kingdom of goodness, righteousness and truth. As this fruit spills out from the inside, we shine brightly and it points others to Christ.

When we try hard in our own efforts to produce this fruit, it can cause others harm. It is part of a false image of who we want to be rather than who we truly are. We do nice things because we want people to look up to us and see us as a good person.

Ever notice this self-effort in some people who work hard to help others? Sometimes their help or support can feel belittling. You feel like an object for their performance rather than an act of genuine love. Someone can say loving things but when their heart is set in another direction, it comes out almost cynical. Or speaking the truth in the name of Jesus comes out critical and hurtful.

To live in the light means to live in the fullness of truth, genuinely and authentically. In this place of humility and vulnerability, we give glory to God. Being false and putting on a front about who we are is living a lie and never brings glory to God.

Because we let the light in, living more authentically, we become more and more passionate and full of life. We bear the fruit of the light which consists in all goodness, righteousness, and truth (Ephesians 5:8).

Jesus says in Luke 6:45 (NCV), "Good people bring good things out of the good stored up in their heart, and evil people bring evil things out of the evil stored up in the heart. For out of the overflow of the heart, the mouth speaks."

In the Message Bible, it says, "It's who you are, not what you say and do, that counts. Your true being brims over into true words and deeds" (Luke 6:45b, MSG).

Love, a fruit of the Spirit, naturally falls from the life that is surrendered to God. Life flows from having a relationship with God and love flows from loving God.

On our own, we have very little to give to others. But with God at the center of our life, we have an unlimited supply of everything that is needed for all God asks of us.

Love. Give everything of yourself. Not for what you can get out of it. Not wasting time on busy work without meaning. But living thoughtfully, with Christ at the center. Love, in all situations. Don't separate parts of your life as secular—know you are called to love in everything. Unrestrained. Not with starts and stops but a continuous flow "fountain of love" that is available for all that need a drink. With no lusts or attached hooks—pure love. The love of devotion to Christ that has nothing to lose and everything to gain. Overcoming obstacles of fear and rejection.

As we are filled with the Spirit, we overflow with the fruit of the Spirit—love, joy, peace, patience, kindness, longsuffering, and self-control. Joy and peace become our countenance even in the hardest times of suffering.

The Spirit of God flows not only in us, bearing fruit in our lives, but through us to the world around us. We will touch other's lives with the life of Christ that dwells within us. It is the natural fruit from living as children of the light.

Colossians 1:27 (NIV) says, "Christ in you, the hope of glory!"

And as children of the light, in humility and trust, we are children of the Spirit. The light is the manifestation of the Spirit. And letting that light work in our lives fills us more and more full of the Spirit of God that we have been born into (2 Cor. 1:21-22) so we shine brightly.

Paul says in 2 Corinthians 3:17-18 (NIV), "Now the Lord is the Spirit, and where the Spirit of the Lord is, there is freedom. And we, who with unveiled faces all reflect the glory of the Lord, are being transformed into His image with intensifying glory, which comes from the Lord, who is the Spirit."

Light up!

To be a light, we need to be filled with the Light. It is God's Spirit shining through us that is the light to the world. The more we reflect His presence and Spirit, the more we shine with His likeness.

Moses came down from the Mountain of God and shined so brightly after spending time face to face with Him, he had to cover his face.

The first time we see the Spirit coming down upon and filling Jesus is in Matthew 3:16-17 when He was baptized. The Spirit came down and rested on Him like a dove. Afterwards, the Spirit led Him into the wilderness for 40 days. Afterwards, He returned to Galilee in the power of the Spirit. News about him spread through the whole countryside. He was teaching in their synagogues, and everyone praised him.

He went to Nazareth, where he had been brought up, and on the Sabbath day he went into the synagogue, as was his custom. He stood up to read, and the scroll of the prophet Isaiah was handed to him. Unrolling it, he found the place where it is written:

'The Spirit of the Lord is on me,
    because he has anointed me
    to proclaim good news to the poor.
He has sent me to proclaim freedom for the prisoners
    and recovery of sight for the blind,
to set the oppressed free,
    to proclaim the year of the Lord's favor.'

Then he rolled up the scroll, gave it back to the attendant and sat down. The eyes of everyone in the synagogue were fastened on him. He began by saying to them, "Today this scripture is fulfilled in your hearing" (Luke 4:14-20, NIV).

A significant part of His purpose while He was on earth was to proclaim the good news, give sight to the blind, heal the lame, set the prisoners free, and release those who were oppressed.

But there is more to it than this. The word *fulfilled* here is the Greek word *pléroó*, Strong's #4137. It means to fill to the full, amply supply or be accomplished. [6] He more than met these promises when He came to earth. He also met these promises through us. We are His legacy.

The scripture in Isaiah 61 (NIV) that Jesus was reading from in the scroll goes on to say,

"…to proclaim the year of the Lord's favor
    and the day of vengeance of our God,
to comfort all who mourn,
    and provide for those who grieve in Zion—

to bestow on them a crown of beauty
    instead of ashes,
the oil of joy
    instead of mourning,
and a garment of praise
    instead of a spirit of despair.
They will be called oaks of righteousness,
    a planting of the Lord
    for the display of his splendor.

They will rebuild the ancient ruins
    and restore the places long devastated;
they will renew the ruined cities
    that have been devastated for generations.
Strangers will shepherd your flocks;
    foreigners will work your fields and vineyards.
And you will be called priests of the Lord,
    you will be named ministers of our God"
(Isaiah 61:2-6).

Notice that the verses move from 'me' to 'they'? Those who have been given so much by Jesus and amply supplied, will carry on the works of the Lord forward. *They* will be the ones who rebuild the devastated places around them for the display of His splendor.

We have been anointed with all we need by the power of the Holy Spirit to carry forward His purposes through our lives. We are His ministers. His purpose becomes our purpose. And in living out this purpose, we display His splendor. We glorify Him.

John 14:12 (NIV) Jesus says, "Very truly I tell you, whoever believes in me will do the works I have been doing, and they will do even greater things than these, because I am going to the Father."

Jesus fulfilled this scripture in a way that amply supplies the Spirit to those who receive Him to perform this work throughout time. He accomplished this for us. It is part of our inheritance from Him. We carry on His legacy.

We may feel helpless in the face of someone going through significant struggles to comfort them or make any kind of difference in their lives. When we don't believe we can make a difference, we may not even try. However, here Jesus is saying that we as His people are anointed to do this work through Him and glorify Him by doing it.

1 John 2:20 (NIV) says, "But you have an anointing from the Holy One, and all of you know the truth."

"How beautiful on the mountains are the feet of those who bring good news, who proclaim peace, who bring good tidings, who proclaim salvation, who say to Zion, 'Your God reigns!'" (Isaiah 52:7, NIV)

Being filled with the Spirit, Jesus would have us live out of the perception that we are His ministers and anointed to carry the works of the Lord forward in delightful anticipation of His will and purposes coming forth.

As we see as He sees, we are in the right spirit (His Spirit) to understand, rebuke and challenge people when needed.

Isaiah 11:4 (AMP) goes on to paint a picture of Jesus seeing clearly from the place of the heart:

> "But with righteousness and justice shall He judge the poor and decide with fairness for the meek, the poor, and the downtrodden of the earth; and He shall smite the earth and the oppressor with the rod [scepter] of His mouth, and with the breath of His lips He shall slay the wicked."

Jesus was never condemning or judgmental to the poor when He walked on the earth. Rather, He looked on them with great mercy. Putting them in their place was elevating them and not putting them down or belittling them. He was an advocate and spoke up for those who could not speak for themselves. He was not against them but with them. And his heart was generous towards them.

In the same way that Jesus went before us in the power of the Spirit, He calls us to follow. Filled with the Spirit of God, we are His hands and feet on the earth. We are anointed to do His will by the power of His Spirit. We are bringers of justice and not judgement to those who are in need.

Lord, help us to be all that You have called us to be. Give us the courage to be authentic and open about who we are. Help us to face our weaknesses and imperfections by being open and vulnerable with those we trust. Give us courage to be uncomfortable without hiding, pretending or covering up our weaknesses. Help us to be people that fully live in the light with others. And give us the humility to not only be real about ourselves, but full of grace for the imperfections and weaknesses of others.

Let us display Your splendor by glorifying You in all we do. Let our lives be filled with Your purposes of bringing Your kingdom and not our own. Free us from doubts about who we are in You. Thank You for all the ways You love us to life.

Have a Good Attitude!

Our outlook, either positive or negative, will have impact our ability to navigate difficulty, the levels of stress in our lives and our overall well-being. Having an optimistic outlook and less worry and stress in our lives is tied closely with both our physical and mental health.

It is proven that a positive outlook and peace of mind has tremendous benefits on our whole system—mind, body and spirit. We will live longer and healthier when we have a positive outlook.

Our minds and thoughts controlled by the Spirit are life and peace (Romans 8:6). Because we as Christians let the light in, allowing it to shape our thoughts and attitudes more like Christ's, we become increasingly passionate and full of life. We also become more optimistic, peaceful and joyful.

As we take on the nature of Christ, we become more like Him in our actions. Having attitudes and thoughts that are aligned with God, the Spirit of God flows not only to us, but through us to the world around us.

So why do we sometimes struggle so greatly living in this flow of the Spirit? Paul says in Romans 7:19 (MSG), "I decide to do good, but I don't *really* do it; I decide not to do bad, but then I do it anyway."

It is our thinking and underlying attitudes that trips us up and gets us off course at times. Our minds, attitudes, and emotions are being renewed. But, this is a process that occurs over time.

Ephesians 4:23-24 (MSG) says, "Everything—and I do mean everything—connected with that old way of life has to go. It's rotten through and through. Get rid of it! And then take on an entirely new way of life—a God-fashioned life, a life renewed from the inside and working itself into your conduct as God accurately reproduces his character in you."

Often where having wrong attitudes and thinking shows up most clearly is in the decanting process. We are bumped into by someone else or experience some difficulty and the mess inside that has not been dealt with spills out.

Our actions and deeds, including our ability to navigate difficulty, are impacted by how we think. And our thinking is based upon our underlying attitudes and assumptions. We believe and then act from our attitudes. Our attitudes are impacted by our framework or the lenses we are looking through.

Luke 11:34-35 says, "Listen, your eye, your outlook, the way you see is your lamp. If your way of seeing is functioning well, then your whole life will be enlightened. But if your way of seeing is darkened, then, then your life will be a dark, dark place. So be careful, people, because your light may be malfunctioning. If your outlook is good, then your whole life will be bright, with no shadowy corners, as when a radiant lamp brightens your home."

When people have been hurt significantly at some point or over a period of time, they can lose their child-like innocence about others. Instead of believing that others have their best intentions at heart, they jump to the conclusion that people are bound to hurt them if they are given a chance. They will close themselves off from vulnerability with others and put up walls to protect themselves.

Sometimes, it is in certain areas where we are wounded that we shut down. Then when someone rubs against us in this area, we react out of our prior hurt rather than out of love. We may not even realize we are reacting out of our past hurts.

How you might spot this in someone else is that you can be going along and suddenly, someone reacts negatively towards something you said or did. You are not sure why or what happened as your intentions were good and they somehow misread you. This usually comes from a deeper place of wounding.

As an example, I once had a woman who sat next to me at work. She had been demoted out of the leadership role that I had been hired to fill. They left her in her same office, next door to me, so as not to not demoralize her further. She was so deeply hurt and angry. When I started my new position, I had no idea of the situation that had happened to her. She was incredibly unkind to me and I didn't understand why. She went out of her way to be hurtful and cruel. And the more I tried to reach out and get along with her, the more she would lash out at me.

One day when I was praying to God about what I could give Him for Christmas, He said to write an apology note to this woman for in any way I may have hurt her and pray for her over the Christmas break. Doing this was not easy for me when she had worked so hard at wounding me.

But, when we returned to work, it was like she was a completely different person. Something happened in her. It was like some of the deep pain was healed. I could see another side of her and found out she could be a very nice person. It was the pain that was causing her to act the way she did towards me. Some months later she even had the opportunity to be in a leadership role again.

We are all broken and bruised and struggle in areas with our attitudes and perceptions. The Beatitudes help us to come outside of ourselves to see differently. Jesus turned people's underlying assumptions and attitudes upside down in Luke 6:20-26 (NIV) when He said,

> "Blessed are you who are poor, for yours is the kingdom of God... But woe to you who are rich, for you have already received your comfort."

Happy are the Broken

It is in our poverty that we see our need for God and His grace. As we are broken over our sin and come to the end of ourselves and our self-sufficiency, we taste more of God in our lives.

We are tempted to think that it is our strengths that make us successful when following God. However, sometimes it is our strengths that make us self-sufficient rather than God-sufficient.

We are also tempted to move into self-righteousness as we compare our strengths to the weaknesses of someone else. The more we feel successful by our own efforts, the less we feel we need God.

In Revelation 3:17 (NIV), Jesus tells the church in Laodicea, "You say, 'I am rich; I have acquired wealth and do not need a thing.' But you do not realize that you are wretched, pitiful, poor, blind and naked."

We learn obedience in being faithful despite our weaknesses. Obedience is not true obedience unless it is coming from a heart of love, trust and worship. Right actions without the right heart result in self-righteousness. True obedience comes from a heart of brokenness instead of self-sufficiency. When we are sufficient on our own, we don't need God and end up doing our activities for Him instead of with Him.

In Luke 18:9-14, Jesus told a story demonstrating what brokenness looks like:

> "Two men went up to the Temple to pray, one a Pharisee, the other a tax man. The Pharisee posed and prayed like this: 'Oh, God, I thank you that I am not like other people—robbers, crooks, adulterers, or, heaven forbid, like this tax man. I fast twice a week and tithe on all my income.'
>
> Meanwhile the tax man, slumped in the shadows, his face in his hands, not daring to look up, said, 'God, give mercy. Forgive me, a sinner.'
>
> Jesus commented, 'This tax man, not the other, went home made right with God. If you walk around with your nose in the air, you're going to end up flat on your face, but if you're content to be simply yourself, you will become more than yourself.'"

It is in authenticity, humility and brokenness that we grow like Christ. Our weaknesses and failures are not imperfections that limit us, they are the very avenue that drives us in desperation and brokenness to greater maturity. It is our weaknesses that help us to grow.

Happy are the Meek

It is in our brokenness that we become meek. Meekness is not the same as weakness. It does not mean going along with everyone and giving up any power you have. Meekness is not being a marshmallow. Rather meekness is about using your power for the good of others in humility. It is a servant's heart rather than a heart to rule over others.

From the beginning, God gave us dominion to serve, tend and care for all He made. What happened in the fall was that our picture of what power looked like became corrupted. What was exceedingly good became full of sin.

God told Adam and Eve in what ways the corruption of sin would bring death. He said in Genesis 3:16-19 that life would be birthed only out of tremendous pain, that there would be lust, and a desire to rule over others rather than serve others out of humility and love. He goes on to tell Adam that his labors would be filled with striving and effort.

"Taking dominion" was twisted from something positive and full of life to something oppressive and diminishing because of the corruption of sin. "Taking dominion" turned negative because sin corrupted these natural motives changing them life giving into a desire to exalt oneself in pride, lust, fear, and self-interest. Very corrupted examples of "taking dominion" include slavery, dictatorships based upon fear, and sex trafficking.

When we love others, we bear God's image in the world. We were intended to be an expression of God in the world that is loving, meek, gentle, kind and full of mercy. We "take dominion" by humbling ourselves, coming under, caring for and empowering others.

Rather than exulting ourselves over others for our own benefit, we lay down our lives and sacrifice so that they may have life. We serve others out of a heart of love that desires their best. This is the way of the meek.

Jesus came into a world that is corrupted with wrong desires, power, self-effort and striving. In the midst of it, He showed us what God had in mind from the beginning and what it looked like to truly "take dominion." He chose twelve disciples that He trained and empowered. He poured His life into them. And He used His power to speak life and give life to all He encountered.

Jesus did not over-run the Romans as the Jews had hoped He would do. Instead, He taught the people about a freedom and joy they could have right amid difficult circumstances. He came underneath people and served them with compassion and mercy.

He humbled Himself as a servant and washed the feet of those He had been given authority over--and called them to do the same, following His example. Then He demonstrated the greatest act of love as He sacrificed Himself for us. For the joy set before Him, He endured the cross with our best interests in mind.

1 John 4:9-11 (HCSB) goes on to say, "God's love was revealed among us in this way: God sent His One and Only Son into the world so that we might live though Him. Love consists in this: not that we loved God, but that He loved us and sent His Son to be the propitiation for our sins. Dear friends, if God loved us in this way, we also must love one another."

Love is at the core of rightly ordered power and dominion. Our expressing God's love is our taking dominion in this world. When we fail to love and we lead or take authority out of any other motive, taking dominion is corrupted.

When we express God's love, we express who He is to the world around us. 1 John 4:12 (AMP) says, "No one has ever seen God. If we love one another, God remains in us and His love is perfected [made complete] in us."

Sometimes in our attempts to love others, we come from the wrong spirit. Rather than letting God's love work through us, we are full of self-effort and striving. With an air of arrogance, we believe that we are the solution and we have the answers that others need. Rather than building bridges in love, we can cause resentment in those we are serving for making untrue assumptions and do more harm than good.

Meekness also involves being teachable like a child. Instead of coming to the table thinking we have all the answers and can solve the problems of others, we come under and learn from others. We let them teach us how to love them and serve them in a way that truly helps and empowers them.

God had a plan for us from the beginning to bear His image in the world. To demonstrate who He is by freely giving His love away to those around us and through self-sacrifice, caring for all that He created. And just like it was in the garden, we come to know God and be like Him through remaining in His love and sharing it with those around us. By sharing it with others, they come to know Him as well.

Happy are the Hungry

It is our brokenness and knowledge of our own poverty, that we cannot make it on our own, which keeps us meek, dependent and hungry for God. Jesus went on in Luke 6:20-26 (NIV) to say, "Blessed are you who hunger now, for you will be satisfied... Woe to you who are well fed now, for you will go hungry."

When we are spiritually hungry, we seek to be filled by God. Our appetites will drive our thoughts and behavior. We will seek what will fill us. Proverbs 16:26 (NASB) says, "The appetite of laborers works for them; their hunger drives them on."

Before I came to the Lord, I remember seeing people who glowed with life and wanting that for myself. I didn't have the same sense of security, adventure or understanding that I was loved as people who were full of life. I longed to glow with life myself but thought it was completely out of my reach. I didn't even know how to relate to people who had lives rich with love, faith and life.

When I came to the Lord, everything changed. I tasted life and His love and it gave me hope. It left me incredibly hungry. This hunger began to drive the choices in my life. As I tasted life and realized it was within my reach, I started making choices to move towards having that life.

Feeding our appetite for God with spiritual food, keeps us hungry for more of God. It also keeps our spirit in tune with God and fills us so that we can pour out to those around us. While feeding our appetite with things of the world, quenches this hunger and dulls our spirits.

As we clutter our hearts and lives up with other things, we begin to look more and more toward distractions to fill us and away from God. He becomes increasingly crowded out. Like King Saul in 1 Samuel 28:6, our spirits become dull and we cannot seem to hear God any longer.

Jesus invites in Isaiah 55:1-3 (NIV), "Come, all you who are thirsty, come to the waters; and you who have no money, come, buy and eat! Come, buy wine and milk without money and without cost. Why spend money on what is not bread, and your labor on what does not satisfy? Listen, listen to Me, and eat what is good, and you will delight in the richest of fare. Give ear and come to Me; listen, that you may live."

Our hunger and brokenness over sin from being sensitive to the Spirit of God, directs us to turn from our old patterns that result in death to new ways that bring life. We begin to live a life of turning from our old ways and habits to His ways.

Happy are the Sad

Jesus says in Luke 6:20, 26 (NIV), "Blessed are you who weep now, for you will laugh... Woe to you who laugh now, for you will mourn and weep."

God is not looking for those who get everything right. He is seeking those who will be quick to repent, turn from their old ways, and learn His ways. In Luke 5:31 (NIV),

Jesus said, "It is not the healthy who need a doctor, but the sick. I have not come to call the righteous, but sinners to repentance."

And in Isaiah 55:7 (NIV) the Lord says, "Let the wicked forsake their ways and the unrighteous their thoughts. Let them turn to the Lord, and he will have mercy on them and to our God, for he will freely pardon."

We come to know the Lord through repenting—realizing our need to turn away from our sin. John's baptism, the baptism of repentance for the remission of sins, prepared the way for the Lord. It opened people's eyes which resulted in them turning from darkness to light, from the power of Satan to God, so that they would receive forgiveness of sins and have a place among the children of light (Acts 16:18).

Repenting, however, is not a one-time event. It needs to be a daily occurrence and part of our regular routine. We walk with God as we are sensitive to His nudges and leadings. Walking in the Spirit as children of the light requires a heart attitude of repentance when God shines the light on an areas of sin.

When we repent, we are being real about what is going on inside. It is counter to pretending and living as our false selves. Too often, we pretend on the outside how we would like to feel on the inside. We hide our mess in the darkness and bury it in shame, refusing to live in the light.

John says in 1 John 1:5-7 (NIV), "This is the message we have heard from Him and declare to you: God is light;

in Him there is no darkness at all. If we claim to have fellowship with Him and yet walk in the darkness, we lie and do not live out the truth. But if we walk in the light, as He is in the light, we have fellowship with one another, and the blood of Jesus, His Son, purifies us from all sin."

Dealing with our sin directly, turning from it and repenting, leads us to new ways of life. We want to diligently keep guard over our hearts, not allowing unrepented sin to take root and harden our hearts, as everything we do flows out from it (Proverbs 4:23).

As we live in the light and are quick to turn and repent from sin, our hearts stay tender towards Him and we have a sense of His presence and joy.

Psalm 16:11 (VOICE) says, "You direct me on the path that leads to a beautiful life. As I walk with You, the pleasures are never-ending, and I know true joy and contentment."

Happy are the Bullied

When we are living in the flow of the Spirit and our hearts and attitudes are right, we can sometimes think that everything will go smoothly for us. We expect that we will somehow avoid hardships and have life easier.

In Luke 6:20-26 (NIV), Jesus says, "Blessed are you when people hate you, when they exclude you and insult you and reject your name as evil, because of the Son of Man. Rejoice in that day and leap for joy, because great is your reward in heaven. For that is how their ancestors treated the prophets...

Woe to you when everyone speaks well of you, for that is how their ancestors treated the false prophets."

And Jesus says in Luke 6:40 (NIV), "A student is not above his teacher, but everyone who is fully trained will be like his teacher."

When we are truly living a life like Jesus, we will be persecuted and rejected at times. Our hunger, thirst, brokenness and tender-heartedness towards God can be like salt in a wound to someone who has fallen away or does not know Christ. The way that we are living may create a sense of conviction in others which makes them uncomfortable. It may confront their behavior and beliefs.

Many of the Christians at the time of Jesus lost their home and everything they knew for following Christ. They were banned from the Synagogue and treated as traitors. Some of them were jailed, beaten or even murdered for their faith in Jesus.

While we live in a country of religious freedom and can be thankful we do not experience this kind of persecution, it still happens through-out the world. Even in America, I have friends who have been banished from family because of their faith.

As we re-arrange our lives around Christ and biblical priorities, we may find that we lose friendships or family relationships we once enjoyed.

People may take offense at our choice to make Christ a high priority in our lives. When we re-arrange our lives around biblical priorities, it will conflict with the ways some others choose to follow.

Matthew 10:34-35 (MSG) says, "Don't think I've come to make life cozy. I've come to cut—make a sharp knife-cut between son and father, daughter and mother, bride and mother-in-law—cut through these cozy domestic arrangements and free you for God. Well-meaning family members can be your worst enemies."

Happy are the Peacemakers

In these difficult circumstances, we need to learn to walk as peacemakers. In Matthew 5:9 (NIV) Jesus says, "Blessed are the peacemakers, for they will be called children of God."

Children, in this case, are those sharing the same nature as their Father. We are reborn and adopted by our heavenly Father. Children naturally imitate their parents and take on their characteristics.

Paul says in Romans 8:28-29 (NIV), "And we know that God works all things together for the good of those who love Him, who are called according to His purpose. For those God foreknew, He also predestined to be conformed to the image of His Son, so that He would be the firstborn among many brothers."

We share the very nature of God and have been predestined and called to demonstrate similar behavior and bear His likeness to the world. In bearing that likeness, we will, just like God, bring true kingdom peace into the world.

Loving one's brother and laying down one's life to serve them does not always mean giving others what they desire. What people desire is not always the best for them. Sometimes engaging in peacemaking creates conflict with others. In some situations, this is the only way to bring true peace. Healthy conflict creates the change that is needed.

Jeremiah was someone who understood healthy conflict. The people of Judah had turned away from God. Jeremiah was given the task by God as prophet to warn the people of the coming judgment of God for their sin in forsaking Him. Shortly after being called, God speaks to Jeremiah in Jer. 1:16-19 (MSG),

> "They'll come and set up headquarters facing Jerusalem's gates, facing all the city walls, facing all the villages of Judah. I'll pronounce my judgment on the people of Judah for walking out on me—what a terrible thing to do!—And courting other gods with their offerings, worshiping as gods sticks they'd carved, stones they'd painted.
>
> But you—up on your feet and get dressed for work! Stand up and say your piece. Say exactly what I tell you to say. Don't pull your punches or I'll pull you out of the lineup.
>
> Stand at attention while I prepare you for your work. I'm making you as impregnable as a castle, immovable as a steel post, solid

> as a concrete block wall. You're a one-man defense system against this culture, against Judah's kings and princes, against the priests and local leaders. They'll fight you, but they won't even scratch you. I'll back you up every inch of the way. God's Decree."

Jeremiah spoke the truth to the people. He spoke of the coming doom and disaster at a time that everything seemed good. The rest of the prophets and priests were speaking peace and prosperity to the people (Jer. 8:11). When life seemed so good, nobody wanted to hear a message of doom. They refused to listen or turn from their evil choices (Jer. 8:15).

Jeremiah's heart in speaking the truth was for the benefit of the people. He was not demanding his own rights or defending himself. He placed himself completely in the hands of God (Jer. 11:20b). He loved the people and carried them in his heart. He grieved over the coming disaster and the great sin of the people.

In lament Jerimiah cries out, "I drown in grief. I'm heartsick. Oh, listen! Please listen! It's the cry of my dear people reverberating through the country. Is God no longer in Zion? Has the King gone away?" (Jer. 8:18-19, MSG)

However, Jeremiah realized that what was needed was not God to relent from the coming disaster as much as the people to turn from their idolatrous ways.

Ultimately, Jeremiah found his joy in being with God, and seeing things God's way. Jeremiah spoke to God, "Just look at the abuse I'm taking! When your words showed up, I ate them—swallowed them whole. What a feast! What delight I took in being yours, O God, God-of-the-Angel-Armies!" (Jeremiah 15:15-17, MSG).

While situations and the circumstances that Jeremiah faced were grim, he had great joy in being with God and following His will. As he spent time with God and followed in His footsteps, He found he shared more and more God's heart, purposes and passions.

God spoke to Jeremiah, "'If you utter worthy, not worthless words, you will be my spokesman. Let this people turn to you, but you must not turn to them. I will make you a wall to this people, a fortified wall of bronze; they will fight against you but will not overcome you, for I am with you to rescue and save you,' declares the Lord" (Jeremiah 15:19-20, NIV).

It is not always easy to speak the truth, but it is always the right thing to do. It takes risking relationships and allowing the consequences to fall to God. It needs to be spoken, even when it confronts others.

At the same time, truth spoken in genuine love and care is not spoken out of harshness, judgement or a desire to belittle someone else. It is delivered in gentleness and humility with a desire to help others.

I greatly value harmony in relationships. However, much of the reason I love harmony is because I get a sense of security from having good feelings in my relationships. I am wired to be motivated by good relationships. On the downside of this is that I seem to look for approval and harmony in my relationships to validate me at times. It results in me going along with others for their approval.

However, one cannot have harmony with what is against God and be walking in His ways. Validating something that we know is harmful and going against God will be detrimental to others, causing them to stumble along further.

Jeremiah loved the people. However, the answer was not for him to become one with them in their sin and go along with their idolatrous plans. If he would have, the people would not have rejected him or tried to kill him. Instead, they would have accepted him, slapping him on the back and including him in their activities.

Jeremiah chose to stand alone. He stood apart from the people, including family, and chose to be with God, speaking the truth in love as the people looked upon him with indignation. He chose standing with God over standing with family relationships and friendships.

Luke 12:52-53 (MSG) says, "I've come to disrupt and confront! From now on, when you find five in a house, it will be—three against two, and two against three; Father against son, and son against father; Mother against daughter, and daughter against mother; Mother-in-law against bride, and bride against mother-in-law."

As the Lord speaks in Jeremiah 17:5-8 (MSG),

> "Cursed is the strong one who depends on mere humans, who thinks he can make it on muscle alone and sets God aside as dead weight. He's like a tumbleweed on the prairie, out of touch with the good earth. He lives rootless and aimless in a land where nothing grows.
>
> But blessed is the man who trusts Me, God, the woman who sticks with God. They're like trees replanted in Eden, putting down roots near the rivers—Never a worry through the hottest of summers, never dropping a leaf, serene and calm through droughts, bearing fresh fruit every season"

The heart is deceitful above all things and desperately sick (Jer. 17:9). We may not even realize it at the time when we are going along with people to keep the peace. For me, because I value harmony, I too easily go along with people.

When I am standing in confrontation with someone, I feel terrible about it and worry about the relationship. Sometimes I can be hard on myself in these situations rather than just trust God with the outcome.

When faced with confrontation, if we try to manage people's behavior and response, it is a form of manipulation that is based in control. We need to speak the truth with kindness and love in our hearts, leaving the outcomes of how people handle it up to God. Like Jeremiah, we need to learn to put ourselves in God's hands.

Being a peacemaker is not the same as being overly nice and agreeable. Being a peacemaker means that we are willing to speak the truth out of love and put the outcomes in the hands of God. The truth spoken in love brings eventual peace. It advances God's kingdom.

Jeremiah's heart in speaking the truth was love for the people and a deep desire to honor God. He genuinely loved the people he was called to serve. He spoke the truth for their benefit, even when they were stubborn-hearted. He trusted that in doing God's will, God would bring about His kingdom purposes.

Sometimes we can fail to speak the truth because we want to feel comfortable and accepted. Then when we do speak the truth, it is out of our own desires and for our own benefit. Speaking the truth becomes about claiming something or controlling someone rather than about helping the other person who is stuck in sin.

James says in James 4:1-2 (MSG), "Where do you think all these appalling wars and quarrels come from? Do you think they just happen? Think again. They come about because you want your own way, and fight for it deep inside yourselves. You lust for what you don't have and are willing to kill to get it. You want what isn't yours and will risk violence to get your hands on it."

Happy are the Merciful

When we speak the truth to others, it needs to be for their benefit and not ours. We need to do it out of a spirit of looking out for their best interests and helping them to grow rather than from a place of judging them, trying to fix them or controlling them for our own interests.

Isaiah 42:3 (NKJV) also says, "A bruised reed shall He not break, and the smoking flax shall He not quench: He shall bring forth judgment unto truth."

The first person to speak always seems right until you hear the other side (Proverbs 18:17). There is always another side of the story. Like the woman who was in pain because she was demoted, there are deeper reasons for behavior we see. Just as mercy is the lens that Jesus sees us through, we need to see others with a lens of mercy.

Rather than judging, we can be curious about what is going on with in someone else's life with a heart to help. Jesus brought forth justice by His own suffering. He did not insist that others got it all right, but rather loved them right where they were.

However, mercy does not mean wishy washy. In expressing mercy, we need to still stand with the truth. The truth said in love never breaks a bruised reed and Jesus was not afraid to speak it. When He healed those who sinned, he told them boldly, "go and sin no more."

Ignoring the truth and pretending all is good when it is not fails to help others go in the right direction. It is not loving. Going along with sin is not the same as mercy. Loving someone off a cliff by encouraging them to continue in sin is failing to love them at all.

Paul confronts the church in 1 Corinthians 5:1 for their wishy-washy attempt at non-judgmental mercy that lacked support of the truth. He says he could hardly believe it was reported to him that a man was sleeping with his father's wife and no one was saying anything about it. The leaders of the church were actually proud of not judging them for their sin. Instead Paul said that they should be stricken with grief and act on it by removing those who were sinning in that way from fellowship (vs. 2).

In speaking the truth, Jesus was not critical and judgmental of people. He believed in the potential of people and called them out into more. When Jesus saw Zacchaeus up in the sycamore tree, Jesus did not criticize or judge him for his past sins, instead, Jesus demonstrated unconditional love and acceptance of him, coming to his house for dinner. Jesus let Zacchaeus know he was valued and delighted in despite his sin.

In speaking the truth in love, this can be difficult with someone in authority. Like the story of the king who was naked and everyone told him how great he looked in his outfit, we can be afraid to speak the truth to someone in authority. It adds an additional element of risk for us.

Jeremiah was an example of someone courageous in speaking to those with authority over him. He spoke on the authority of God. He had no doubt where his authority was coming from. He spoke to kings, elders, head priests and others with boldness.

In Jeremiah 22:1-3 (MSG), the Lord said to Jeremiah, "God's orders: Go to the royal palace and deliver this Message. Say, 'Listen to what God says, O King of Judah, you who sit on David's throne—you and your officials and all the people who go in and out of these palace gates. This is God's Message: Attend to matters of justice. Set things right between people. Rescue victims from their exploiters. Don't take advantage of the homeless, the orphans, the widows. Stop the murdering!'"

When it comes to people in authority, we need to humbly keep our motives in check, but still must be willing to speak the truth in love when it is needed. In doing so, it is best for both them and for ourselves.

Peter says in 1 Peter 2:13, 18 (NASB) "Submit yourselves for the Lord's sake to every human institution, whether to a king as the one in authority, or to governors as sent by him Servants, be submissive to your masters with all respect, not only to those who are good and gentle, but also to those who are unreasonable."

Being subject or in submission does not mean to go along with evil. We are to honor everyone (1 Peter 2:17). However, it is not honoring to yourself or anyone to go along with someone in doing wrong. It means to respectfully speak the truth in love and trust the consequences to God.

Jesus says in Matthew 15:14 (NKJV), "And if the blind lead the blind, both shall fall into the ditch." Instead of following along, with gentleness and respect, it is the kind thing to do to speak the truth.

And what if the one in authority does not agree?

As an example from the Bible, when David ordered a census in Israel, Joab knew it was wrong and pleaded with the king not to go ahead with it. However, "the king's word prevailed against Joab" and they performed the census (2 Samuel 24:4). The result was devastating. There was pestilence on Israel, killing 70,000 men. Ultimately, Joab had the choice of not performing the census which may have resulted in serious personal consequences to him, or as he did, go along with the orders which resulted in serious consequences to a multitude of others.

Going along with someone's orders when it is wrong does not bear good fruit. Proverbs 25:26 (NIV) says "Like a muddied spring or a polluted well is a righteous man who gives way to the wicked."

Happy are the Pure Hearted

Romans 6:13-14 (NKJV) says, "And do not present your members as instruments of unrighteousness to sin, but present yourselves to God as being alive from the dead, and your members as instruments of righteousness to God. For sin shall not have dominion over you, for you are not under law but under grace."

To *present* is the Greek word *paristemi*, Strong's #3936. It also translates as yield. It means to place a person or thing at one's disposal. [7] We are to yield ourselves to God, putting ourselves at His disposal as "instruments of righteousness to God."

To *yield*, according to the Nelson's Topical Bible Index means to produce or to surrender. [8] It is not something we do by our own effort but is brought forth because of cooperating with God's Spirit. To produce here means to bear fruit or bring forth from the inside out.

It is used in Genesis 1:11-12 (NKJV) where God said, "Let the earth bring forth grass, the herb yielding seed, and the fruit tree yielding fruit after his kind, whose seed is in itself, upon the earth: and it was so. And the earth brought forth grass, and herb yielding seed after his kind, and the tree yielding fruit, whose seed was in itself, after his kind: and God saw that it was good."

And Paul says in Romans 11:16-18 (NKJV), "For if the firstfruit is holy, the lump is also holy; and if the root is holy, so are the branches. And if some of the branches were broken off, and you, being a wild olive tree, were grafted in among them, and with them became a partaker of the root and fatness of the olive tree, do not boast against the branches. But if you do boast, remember that you do not support the root, but the root supports you."

We have been grafted into Jesus, as a branch is grafted onto the root of a tree. Therefore, as we yield to Him, we produce fruit after His kind—holiness. Holiness is not something we produce by following the law or trying to conform to certain behaviors or practices. This only results in self-righteousness.

Many of the Israelites were full of self-righteousness. They knew the law and tried to conform to the law in their own strength. Paul says in Romans 10:3-4 (NKJV), "For they [Israel] being ignorant of God's righteousness, and seeking to establish their own righteousness, have not submitted to the righteousness of God. For Christ is the end of the law for righteousness to everyone who believes."

Jesus says in Matthew 5:20 (NIV), "For I tell you that unless your righteousness surpasses that of the Pharisees and the teachers of the law, you will certainly not enter the kingdom of heaven."

We obtain righteousness—right standing with God—by our faith in God. Paul says in Romans 10:10 (NASB), "For with the heart a person believes, resulting in righteousness, and with the mouth he confesses, resulting in salvation."

And holiness is produced as we present or yield ourselves to God, allowing Him to bear His fruit in our lives. It is not conforming our actions to the law that make us holy but our willingness to allow God to transform us from the inside out—our surrender.

Paul says in Romans 12:1-2 (NKJV), "I beseech you therefore, brethren, by the mercies of God, that you present your bodies a living sacrifice, holy, acceptable to God, which is your reasonable service. And do not be conformed to this world, but be transformed by the renewing of your mind, that you may prove what is that good and acceptable perfect will of God."

To present or to yield can also mean to bring near in fellowship or intimacy [8]. It is as we draw near to God in devotion to Him that we are yielded and transformed from the inside out more into His likeness.

Amos 3:3 (NKJV) asks, "Can two walk together, except they be agreed?" We draw near to God by agreeing in our hearts with Him. We obey Him, yielding to His will out of love and reverence.

Jesus says in John 15:10 (NLT), "If you obey my commands, you will remain in My love, just as I have obeyed my Father's commands and remain in His love."

This is different than trying to follow the law in our own strength, which cannot bear fruit in our lives because we are not abiding in the Vine (John 15:4). Romans 7:6 (NIV) says, "But now, by dying to what once bound us, we have been released from the law so that we serve in the new way of the Spirit, and not in the old way of the written code."

In Romans 6:15-19, Paul speaks of choosing to be slaves to sin or to righteousness. We *choose* whom we present ourselves slaves to obey—sin that leads to death or obedience leading to righteousness. He goes on to say, having obeyed from the heart the form of doctrine to which we were delivered, we have been set free from sin and became slaves of righteousness for holiness.

Slave here is the Greek word *doulos*, which means servant or "one who gives himself up to the will of another." [9] We make ourselves slaves by giving our will over to what our heart is devoted to.

The path to holiness is one of whole-hearted devotion to God and not one of conforming our behaviors to the law. We are not more holy for following rules. What makes us holy is God as we surrender our hearts in full devotion.

Holiness, the Greek word *hagiosune*, Strong's #42, is demonstrated by our actual conduct. [10] But it flows out of our heart devotion. Conformity comes externally from pressures outside, while transformation into greater holiness is rooted in our devotion on the inside. It comes from our hearts.

The results of holiness do not look the same as with conformity which is about getting all the actions right. Like the face of Moses after spending time with God on the mountain, holiness shines from the inside out.

Jesus tells his disciples that when the tares are gathered and burned in the fire so that all that is left is pure, "Then the righteous will shine forth as the sun in the kingdom of their Father" (Matthew 13:43, NKJV).

True holiness will shine forth from the inside out. It draws and points others to God. Conformity is about fitting in and being accepted. It is like perfectionism, which is about looking good. We are seeking to be appreciated or accepted, drawing people to us, rather than pointing them to God.

Conformity is the result of our own comparisons with others. When we are always comparing ourselves to others, we go back and forth between being filled with pride for being better than others or feeling inadequate for being not as good as others.

Competing, comparing, and conforming derail us from entering the fullness of what God has for us. It leaves us discontent and dissatisfied with ourselves and others. We cannot be fulfilled and content when we are comparing ourselves with others. We are only truly fulfilled as we become who God created us to be.

God desires us to be content in fulfilling our purpose in Him. 1 Timothy 6:6 (NKJV) says, "But godliness with contentment is great gain." We need to embrace who God made us to be individually and allow Him to transform us more and more into this. This process happens as we set our hearts to seek God in devotion.

God has a unique plan and design for each one of us. He formed us in our mother's womb with our purpose and calling in mind. Before any of our days are lived out, He planned each one of them.

However, we cannot achieve our purpose and calling by striving externally to make it happen. In striving in our own effort, we usually leave dead bodies in our wake. As an example, Moses first killed an Egyptian with his bare hands and buried him before fulfilling his call 40 years later led by God to bring the Israelites out of captivity.

Striving to achieve what we think is our calling and how it should look is based on our own expectations. This is not the same as yielding to God. When we strive to obtain our identity, even when we think it is what God has called us to be, we will find ourselves conforming to our own and others' expectations rather than experiencing true transformation.

As we yield to God, we will find He calls us into a greater purpose than we can imagine. And rooted in that purpose is sacrificial love. Love is the basis for genuine holiness. Without love for others, we are like a clanging symbol or a noisy gong (1 Cor. 13:1). As Paul notes in 1 Corinthians 13, we have nothing, gain nothing and are nothing outside of love. Love is the core of a full life.

We learn to love each other not by comparing, competing or trying to be like each other, but by complimenting each other, encouraging each other, and making room for each other's gifts.

God in His great wisdom, not only forms us uniquely for our calling, but then places us among others who are uniquely different so that we can learn to love each other.

Paul says in Romans 12:3-5 (NKJV), "For I say, through the grace given to me, to everyone who is among you, not to think of himself more highly than he ought to think, but to think soberly, as God has dealt to each one a measure of faith. For as we have many members in one body, but all members do not have the same function, so we, being many, are one body in Christ, and individually members of one another."

God has created space for us to use our unique gifts to add value to others within the body of Christ. Paul tells the church in 1 Corinthians 12:12-14 (NKJV), "For as the body is one and has many members, but all the members of that one body, being many, are one body, so also is Christ. For in fact the body is not one member but many."

Unity within the body of Christ does not come about by people coming together in a group and holding hands. While this kind of community is sweet, and can lead to greater unity of heart, full unity comes about as each person, with their unique gifts, comes into line with the purposes of God for their lives and into line with their position within the body of Christ.

The ear, nose, mouth, foot, hand, elbow, and knee all come into alignment with each other as they are receiving the essential blood that is pumped from the heart (Christ). Each person steps into their individual position, submitting to each other out of reverence for Christ (Eph. 5:21). And at the same time, they appreciate, value, encourage and make room for the gifts of their brother.

When the body comes together as one with all its diversity, this is unity. We are not comparing, conforming or trying to fit in to look like everyone else; but rather all becoming who God has made us uniquely to be. As we step into our position using the gifts God gave us and how He wired us, we fit together with others as one.

Paul goes on to say in Romans 12:6-8 (NKJV), "Having then gifts differing according to the grace that is given to us, let us use them: if prophecy, let us prophesy in proportion to our faith; or ministry, let us use it in our ministering; he who teaches, in teaching; he who exhorts, in exhortation; he who gives, with liberality; he who leads, with diligence; he who shows mercy, with cheerfulness."

When each person comes in line using their own unique gifts to serve each other, the whole body is built up for the benefit of all. Paul says in 1 Corinthians 12:4-7 (NKJV), "Now there are different gifts, but the same Spirit. And there are different ministries, but the same Lord. And there are different results, but the same God who produces all of them in everyone. To each person the manifestation of the Spirit is given for the benefit of all."

Each person is coming alive to God's purposes, being transformed from the inside out. The Holy Spirit knitting the body together through love as He manifests His gifts uniquely through each one for the self-sacrificing benefit of all. And Christ is at the head, directing, leading and causing the body to grow with the increase that is from God (Eph. 5:25-27). This is the holy Bride of Christ who has begun to make herself ready (Rev. 19:7).

We are to complement each other and build each other up. Paul says in Ephesians 5:29 (NKJV), "For no one ever hated his own flesh, but nourishes and cherishes it, just as the Lord does the church. For we are members of His body, of His flesh and of His bones."

The fruit of devotion to God which leads to holiness is always love. We cannot have true holiness apart from love so we cannot have holiness outside of community.

Paul writes in Romans 13:8 (NKJV), "Owe no one anything except to love one another, for he who loves another has fulfilled the law."

Paul paints a picture of what holiness and love looks like in Romans 12:9-10 (NKJV). He writes, "Let love be without hypocrisy. Abhor what is evil. Cling to what is good. Be kindly affectionate to one another with brotherly love, in honor giving preference to one another."

Whenever we compete, compare, or try to get ahead of others, we are not walking in brotherly love. Rather, love looks to help others connect with God's purposes so they can become all God has for them to be. We see others through the eyes of God as holy onto Him and desire for them to flourish.

Rather than compare and compete, we complement each other and build each other up. Paul says in Ephesians 5:29 (NKJV), "For no one ever hated his own flesh, but nourishes and cherishes it, just as the Lord does the church. For we are members of His body, of His flesh and of His bones."

In Romans 14:19 (NKJV) he says, "Therefore let us pursue the things which make for peace and the things by which one can edify another." And in Romans 15:2 he says, "Let each of us please his neighbor for his good, leading to edification."

It is the ones who spend their energies to invest themselves in humbly serving others rather than concerning themselves with their own success that Jesus calls the greatest. He says in Matthew 23:11 (NKJV), "The greatest among you will be your servant."

Lord, thank You for the gift of the Beatitudes. Help us to walk them out in our day to day lives. Empower us to bring Your kingdom to every difficult and chaotic circumstance. Let us be those who daily take up our cross, deny ourselves and follow You.

Give us wisdom to know when to speak the truth, the courage to stand strong in it, and the kindness and goodness needed to deliver it in love.

Dance for Joy!

The freedom to play, celebrate, and use our creative abilities are gifts of God's goodness to us. They are part of coming to life. Creating, singing, playing and celebrating are gifts that were given as image bearers of God. They reflect Him.

I love the way one children's author writes of God in the scene of creation,

> "Dance!
> In the beginning, God sang everything into being—for the joy of it—and set the whole universe dancing.
> God was in the center, at the heart of everything." [11]

The author refers to Job 38:7, "The morning stars sang together, and the sons of God shouted for joy."

Zephaniah 3:17 (NASB) gives us a picture of a joyful and playful God, "The Lord your God is in your midst, A victorious warrior. He will exult over you with joy, He will be quiet in His love, He will rejoice over you with shouts of joy."

In Jeremiah 31:4 (NLT) he tells the people who were experiencing God's judgment, "You will again be happy and dance."

The natural state of creation is joy bursting into life and flourishing. In a children's Bible this author writes about God creating the earth:

> "'Hello trees!' God said. 'Hello grass and flowers!' And everything everywhere burst into life. He made buds bud; shoots shoot; flowers flower. 'You are good,' God said. And they were." [12]

Being in God's presence and walking with Him, we will more and more come to life in our creative abilities and gifts He has given to us. We will become more and more who we were made to be. One of the fruits of His Spirit in our lives is joy. As we experience His pleasure in us and His presence, our hearts fill with joy.

David says in Psalm 92:12-14 (NASB), "The righteous man will flourish like the palm tree, he will grow like a cedar in Lebanon. They are planted in the house of the Lord; they flourish in the courts of our God. They will still yield fruit in old age; They shall be full of sap and very green."

To flourish means to blossom profusely. Like Aaron's rod the budded, which not only sprouted but brought forth blossoms and ripe olives, when we are standing with God in the place that He has called us, we will thrive internally as well as externally in what we have available to give and pour out on others. We will burst forth with life from the inside out.

We must be connected to the Vine who causes us to flourish so the work we do will have kingdom impact. As we trust and look to Jesus with an open heart, we come into position. When we are faithful in all the small things He gives us along the way and we step out in faith where He speaks to step, we will bear fruit. This fruit is not the fruit of self-effort but powerful kingdom fruit that pushes out from within because of the work He has done in us.

Bearing fruit overflows in our life in abundant generosity—both to us and through us to others. Deuteronomy 15:10 (NIV) says, "Give generously to them [the poor] and do so without a grudging heart; then because of this the Lord your God will bless you in all your work and in everything you put your hand to."

Spiritual maturity is not measured by us getting the actions right and following rules. Rather, it is measured by our representation of Jesus to the world as the body of Christ in unity with others.

We bear the fruit of the kingdom as we are tied to the Vine and, in connection with others, love and serve each other and those around us. We flourish and are most alive when we come into alignment with others and use our gifts, resources and energies to love others in the unique way that God designed us. This is the dance we are in.

One person writes about spiritual dancing:

> "I only had to realize that I always did, as the greatest 'Dancer' of All, dances through me. And I needed to learn to allow, once again; to stop fighting the flow any more, to simply learn to play along with the melody of life, and that is when I began to dance!
>
> And soon it took me to places I could have never visited on my own, the darkest and brightest corners of my being and that of the universe.
>
> This dance is but a mighty river of joy when we choose to dance along to its flow. Your every cell knows it, when you are dancing with the flow, as it is born out of this flow.
>
> Yet there is great stillness in this dance, an immense awareness of the presence, and sweet occurrences of synchronicity only add to the sweetness of this giant reservoir of love, that life itself is." [13]

Paul writes in Galatians 3:11-12 (MSG), "The person who lives in right relationship with God does it by embracing what God arranges for him. Doing things for God is the opposite of entering into what God does for you."

Jesus lived serving and giving His life away to others out of the overflow of fully living in the love of His Father and fully being who His Father called Him to be. He also did this in community with others, sharing this passion and His life with those around Him. In this place of giving His life away, building others up, living in community, and serving others out of the overflow of love, He had tremendous joy in the sacrifice.

Hebrews 12:2 (NASB) says, "fixing our eyes on Jesus, the author and perfecter of faith, who for the joy set before Him endured the cross, despising the shame, and has sat down at the right hand of the throne of God."

In John 15:9-13 (NIV), Jesus tells His disciples, "As the Father has loved Me, so have I loved you. Now remain in My love. If you keep My commands, you will remain in My love, just as I have kept My Father's commands and remain in His love. I have told you this so that My joy may be in you and that your joy may be complete. My command is this: Love each other as I have loved you. Greater love has no one than this: to lay down one's life for one's friends."

In this place of freely giving away our lives to others in sacrificial service, out of the overflow of love from Jesus, we flourish. We enter the flow of this dance with God that gives ourselves away for others. We experience freedom, peace, and overflowing joy as we are filled with sacrificial love for those around us. We have a deep sense of purpose.

It does not mean that life is easy or flows along with no difficulties, but it does mean that those difficulties will draw us closer to God rather than further away from Him.

I think of a parent raising a child with significant special needs. They may work tirelessly behind the scenes day in and day out giving their life sacrificially to love and ease the struggle of their child. Because the demands are so high, they may give up a career and dreams they had for themselves to be there for their child and meet their needs. Yet there is purpose, meaning and joy along the path and in community with others who come around them. God sees and delights in their faithfulness.

Flourishing while being faithful following God's will is the opposite of being very disciplined, gritting our teeth and doing what we are supposed to do in a legalistic manner. Doing what we think we are supposed to do and what will make us look good is rooted in presenting a false image.

There is no room for the false self in the place of flourishing in our calling. The false self is an illusion based upon us covering up and hiding who we really are. Living falsely makes us feel more empty, afraid and alone. Living as our true selves in our true lives, opens us up to more of God and others around us.

Paul says in Philippians 2: 1-4 (MSG), "If you've gotten anything at all out of following Christ, if his love has made any difference in your life, if being in a community of the Spirit means anything to you, if you have a heart, if you care—then do me a favor: Agree with each other, love each other, be deep-spirited friends. Don't push your way to the front; don't sweet-talk your way to the top. Put yourself aside, and help others get ahead. Don't be obsessed with getting your own advantage. Forget yourselves long enough to lend a helping hand."

It is as we remain connected to God that a life of flourishing is possible. Jesus came that we may have life abundantly (John 10:10). To enter the flow of the abundant life, we need to fully surrender our hearts to God and let Him lead. We open our hands and our hearts wide to God and hold things in the world loosely.

Jesus says in Mark 8:34 (MSG), "Anyone who intends to come with Me has to let Me lead. You're not in the driver's seat; I am. Don't run from suffering; embrace it. Follow Me and I'll show you how. Self-help is no help at all. Self-sacrifice is the way, My way, to saving yourself, your true self."

Jesus is fully capable of leading. We listen to the melody in our hearts and dance with Him to the beat. We do not enter the flow of the dance half-heartedly but put our all into it. Sometimes this dance can take dives and swirls we never expected. When it does, we hold tight to Jesus and don't let go.

Derailers – Joy Stealers

It is God who created us, formed us and gave us our desires and passion. When we lay them before Him, He will purify them and use them in answering our call. However, even godly desires can get distorted when we put them before our relationship with Jesus.

David desired to be king, but he never grasped for it. Instead, he embraced the path that God had for him, entering the flow of the river and allowing the current to form and shape him for his eventual rule. Had David chose ruling, like Saul, above his relationship with Jesus, he would have sold his very soul for something hollow, shallow, and void of life. He realized kingship had no value on its own.

Whenever we put something else before God it will derail us from the flow of this dance and cause us to trip up. As we stumble, we often try to regain control which further sends us off course. This dance is one of full surrender as in Song of Solomon 8:3 (NIV), "His left arm is under my head and his right arm embraces me."

As with Lot's wife who looked back and turned into a pillar of salt, looking back at past successes or failures can also derail us. We cannot be looking back and at the same time be moving forward.

When Moses led the Israelites out of Egypt, they continually looked back and started complaining. Instead of entering into what God had for them now, they compared and complained about those things they left behind. They began to make Egypt, a place of their bondage, an idol.

We need to let go of what is in the past and say yes to what God has for us now. Philippians 3:13-14 (NIV) says, "Brothers and sisters, I do not consider myself yet to have taken hold of it. But one thing I do: Forgetting what is behind and straining toward what is ahead, I press on toward the goal to win the prize for which God has called me heavenward in Christ Jesus."

Being critical and ungrateful is also something that will cause us to stumble. Rather than receiving what God has before us as a gift, we compare and complain, leaving us in greater want. What we have is never enough. We miss the gifts that God has for us in the moment by being critical.

Television can cause us to compare and want more. Shows are designed with product placement to create a desire for them. Commercials are filled with all the stuff we somehow can't live without. People are full of charisma and have just the right things to say all the time.

Reality is that there are no perfect people who have everything. And when they do have everything material but lack Jesus, they feel empty inside. If we are looking for it, there is always something to be critical about and the grass will always look greener in some ways on the other side.

We can let go of our expectations of being perfect, having the perfect life, and surrounding ourselves with perfect people. The joy is in how God uses imperfect people with weaknesses to do His will. We do not need to keep striving to have more or be more. God will use us just as we are if our hands are open and we are willing.

Paul says in Philippians 4:8 (NIV), "Finally, brothers and sisters, whatever is true, whatever is noble, whatever is right, whatever is pure, whatever is lovely, whatever is admirable—if anything is excellent or praiseworthy—think about such things and the God of peace will be with you."

Sometimes it is our fears over what might happen or our trying to figure things all out due to lack of trust that causes unrest in our life. We can expect the worst to happen rather than the best. Projecting difficulty steals our joy, peace and rest. Our negative thoughts take us to a place of striving to be in control and manage our circumstances out of fear, anxiety and being troubled.

Difficulties in our life or losing something or someone we value can bring us to a place of anticipating the worst. Rather than seeing God's care through our difficulties, we fear disaster. We feel all alone in our troubles. When I used to struggle with a fear of disaster from difficulties that arose, I wrote the following poem in a conversation with God:

Child,
Disaster is not what I have planned for you.
But to love, and see you through
Falling you will do into my arms
Not into disaster or into harm
Learn to treasure that moments that are now
Trusting my love will show you how
Let your life speak of my goodness and care
Let my mercy fall and meet you there
My goodness is new every day
Let go of your worries and let me wash your frets away.

Worry is like a weed that grows. If we feed it, it will choke out the life of God and the work He is doing in us. Rather than being free to flourish and thrive, we will be bound by our thoughts and fears.

In Matthew 6:25 (NIV) Jesus tells us, "Therefore I tell you, do not worry about your life, what you will eat or drink; or about your body, what you will wear. Is not life more than food, and the body more than clothes?"

Worry is rooted in fear of what will happen. Living and acting out of fears like worry choke out the life of God in our lives. They keep us striving and driven, full of anxiety rather than acting from the heart. We cannot be creative, play or come alive when we are in bound by fear and anxiety.

When I was a new Christian, God spoke to me through another poem I wrote in a conversation with Him. At the time, I didn't know the first thing about who God created me to be. Fear, a need for security and for approval kept me striving to please Him and others rather than coming alive to the purposes He had for me. Perfect love drives out all fear (1 John 4:18). But I only knew His love in my head, and understood it very little in my heart.

Here is that poem—

Precious Daughter,
It won't be long before you'll see,
Just how worthwhile you are to me.
You are precious and cherished in my sight,
Watching you grow is my delight!
You may stumble along the way,
But your worth is determined by the price I paid –

My Son's death on the cross, so you would know,
How it is I love you so.
Quit rating your worth on what you do,
And searching others eyes to value you.
You are already worthwhile in my eyes,
Turn to me and let go of the lies.
I have my purpose, and my plan,
I won't let you fall out of my hand.

You were forged from the love in my heart,
Looking at you, my eyes never part.
What makes you worthwhile, worthy to love?
You are a precious creation, made from above.
You are filled with good things from my treasure chest,
For you my dear, I desire the best.
Discovery is half of the fun,
As we walk this road, you and I as one.
I do have a plan for you in store,
As you mature, you will see more.
Be patient, my dear, and hold out your hand,
As we walk forward into the Promised Land.

As I have gained more and more confidence in His love for me over the years, a great deal of the fear and need for security from my environment has been driven out. And as I am free from the fear, striving to please, seeking approval, and looking for security, I am more and more free to come alive in Him to His purposes. And I am much more at peace.

Sometimes it is not worry or fear, but being overly busy that takes us from a place of rest. We hurriedly go from activity to activity and do not take the time to slow down. Often, it can be really good activities that we are doing *for God* so we justify it to ourselves that we are doing the right things.

When the needs around us are high, we can think we are responsible to fill all of them. It is important to know who God made us uniquely so that we say yes to the right activities. We do not want to fill up our schedule with doing things for God rather than embracing what He has for us.

Rather than being led by the Spirit we are driven by our own sense of responsibility and being needed. We live in a culture where we are valued by what we produce and do with our time. We also may desire to please others and live up to expectations they are putting on us.

Whenever we are driven by expectations, whether they are our own or someone else's, we will be drained and eventually burn out. Our activities will leave us feeling empty. We become tired and weary in doing too much because the things we are doing are based in misplaced motives rather than surrender to God.

Blame is another attitude that can get us in trouble and steal our joy. Blaming someone for our circumstances has accusation behind it and imprisons us. It turns us into the victim and disempowers us in moving forward.

We can trust that God will use our situations, no matter how difficult, for our good. When we blame, instead of trusting God and asking Him for what He might have for us, we are only looking at what 'happened to us' in a negative light. We make ourselves a victim in the story.

Esau is an example of someone who blamed his brother. He did not want to take responsibility for the lack of love in his heart for God that caused him to lose blessings in his life.

When his brother Jacob stole his blessings, Esau blamed Jacob and saw himself as the victim. He told himself that it was his brother Jacob's fault for stealing the blessings from God out of his life. As a result, he was caught in a trap of anger and victimization that resulted in him becoming stuck. Esau even threatened to kill his brother.

Esau's anger toward his brother for the circumstances, that were really the result of his own weak heart towards God, caused him to be stuck. It was this victim attitude that gave his brother Jacob power to rule over him. It was not until Jacob fled for his life and went to live with the uncle Lebanon that Esau was able to start to mature, take responsibility for his relationship with God and gain freedom.

Esau thought, by birth, he was part of the kingdom of God and entitled to its benefits as a right of first in birth order. When his brother stole them, he blamed his brother and complained about not getting what he was entitled to receive. Yet, he never really valued it.

Esau sought his fulfillment from the world around him instead of from God. Jacob, on the other hand, desperately sought an eternal kingdom. While he went about it in a manipulative way, what Jacob desired was ultimately a walk with God. The stew that Esau sold his birthright to Jacob for, was the evidence of what was in Esau's heart. Esau asked what good his birthright was if he was starving of hunger so he traded. Esau thought little of his relationship to God and cared much more for his immediate fulfillment.

Envy is another derailer. Whenever we are looking at someone else and comparing, we are going to stumble. Envy causes us to self-centeredly compare ourselves with someone else with a desire that they would have less and we would have more.

James 3:13-16 (GW) says, "Do any of you have wisdom and insight? Show this by living the right way with the humility that comes from wisdom. But if you are bitterly jealous and filled with self-centered ambition, don't brag. Don't say that you are wise when it isn't true. That kind of wisdom doesn't come from above. It belongs to this world. It is self-centered and demonic. Wherever there is jealously and rivalry, there is disorder and every kind of evil."

Envy and self-seeking are closely tied together. They are often grouped as one in the same because selfishness is at the root of envy. Paul says in 2 Corinthians 12:20 (NLT), "For I am afraid that when I come I won't like what I find, and you won't like my response. I am afraid that I will find quarreling, jealousy, anger, selfishness, slander, gossip, arrogance, and disorderly behavior."

While envy and jealousy sound horrible, they often are not quickly or easily identified as such. We react to a situation without realizing that we are acting out of envy. Like in the cases from the Bible, the situation often feels very unfair to the person who is jealous.

Like the older brother in the story of the Prodigal Son, we may have labored for years for something, being faithful and paying the price in the heat of the day, but then see someone else come along and reap the same benefits. When something like this happens, we may feel unfairly treated and overlooked.

Or like with Joseph and his brothers when he was young, someone throws us under the bus a few times and makes us look bad to appear better than us. Then they are favored as a result and we pay the price from their bad report. Consequently, we resent them for it.

Or like with Saul, we trained someone up, invested heavily and developed them only to find that they are exceptionally talented and gifted. So much so that we fade in the background as everyone acknowledges them. They gladly take all the glory and we begin to resent that we put ourselves there by the opportunities we provided them and by mentoring them.

Often envy has a sense of unfairness about it. We feel wronged in some way. There is also fear and self-protection behind it. We may feel justified when choosing envy because of the sense of unfairness and a feeling of a need to protect ourselves from harm. However, when we choose envy, we make a choice for grasping something over loving someone. The 'something' we desire becomes more important than valuing the 'someone.'

Envy is rooted in idolizing circumstances. We want something that someone else has. We not only want it for ourselves, but we do not have any joy in them having what we want. It is void of love and does not desire the best for another.

In a spirit of envy, we will try to manipulate or control our circumstances to wield it in our benefit. Rather than being open-handed, our fists become clenched tight around what we desire. Saul struggled with this when it came to being king and being admired.

Like with Saul, if we do not deal with our feelings of envy and jealousy, they may ultimately totally derail us (Romans 2:8). Saul lost sight of God as He gripped tightly to what he desired. His life spiraled further and further into darkness as he made worse and worse choices of murder and being led by divination that had been banned by his own order earlier. Hosea 8:7 (NASB) says, "For they sow the wind and they reap the whirlwind."

What helps us to deal with our struggles with criticalness, ingratitude, worry, blame, and envy is not working harder to eliminate them. As we work harder, we often find we become more stuck in them. While derailers will cause us to get off track, it is practicing spiritual disciplines that will help us gain freedom from them.

The purpose of spiritual disciplines is to connect us with God so we can be filled with His presence. In this place we are strengthened in our walk and given the power to overcome derailers. Spiritual disciplines draw us closer to God and cause us to flourish.

Spiritual disciplines can take many different forms. Because of the way we are wired or the season in our lives, some spiritual disciplines naturally draw us to connect with God with ease while others may seem hard for us.

For example, being a natural introvert, I connect with getting away for some quiet time to read the Word and reflect. While someone who is highly active and energetic, may deeply connect with God while running or gardening.

It is not so much the activity itself that is the key but the purpose of the activity in connecting us with God in a deeper way. Like using an icon, the purpose of any spiritual discipline is to point us to God and help our hearts connect so that we can be filled to overflowing and give out to those around us.

For me, as an empty nester, there was a time I would spend a Sabbath day every week with God praying, reading the Word and writing. Now that I have kids again and my elderly mother living with me, this is not realistic for me.

My places of deep connection are times with my kids before bed where we read and act out the Word together. Or when we are singing a worship song together. Also in doing devotionals with my mother. I find these times very nurturing to my spiritual walk.

Gratitude is also a practice that will connect us with God and fill us. If we struggle with a critical attitude, worry, fear, blame or envy, we are looking at others or the circumstances around us with squinty eyes. We have a scarcity mentality that it is not enough, we are not enough and others are not enough.

Practicing gratitude is a great discipline to help guide us off that path and back to God. When we are looking at all the gifts that God has provided, it opens our hearts back up to the abundance that has been poured out upon us. We remember that God is good, all that He does is good and all that He has provided is good.

It is when we are filled that we have capacity to give back out to others around us. To be fully alive in Him is to use what God has given to us in resources, time, and unique gifts to love others. Out of the passion and the desires of our heart, we use our unique gifts to love others well and help them in being their greatest version of themselves. It is in living out God's calling for our life that we will find real life, peace and contentment, even amid difficulties, storms, and challenge.

There was nothing Paul would rather do than preach the gospel. He also had a huge passion for the Gentiles to know Christ. When he brought the Gospel to unreached areas, it caused others to come to know Christ, grow and flourish. At the same time, Paul came fully alive in doing this. He flourished because it was in him.

This didn't mean his calling or his life was easy. He endured great difficulties and spent time in prison for doing what he was called to do. He could endure and weather the storms because he was doing with Jesus what he was most passionate about. He was fulfilling His calling.

Sometimes we can think that if something is easy for us, then this determines our calling. But if we only do those things which come easy to us or give up as soon as something is difficult, we will never grow in new ways. It is our passion about something that helps us press through the difficulties.

We put our hands to what our hearts prompt as we trust that Jesus will support us and sustain us. At the same time, where we are called has a great deal with how we are wired. For example, Paul was energized in going to new places and preaching the gospel. He could do it repeatedly without becoming weary. While someone else who is not called to this, would be totally drained by the same experiences.

Father, thank You that You have created each one of us with individual desires and unique gifts that You call us to use as we enter into the dance with You. I love the thought that a dance is intimate, one-to-one, and face-to-face. There is nothing we would rather do in this life than dance with You. Draw us into this dance. And let us be swept up in Your grace as we learn and grow, letting You lead.

Tag, You're It!

When Jesus, moved into the neighborhood, He brought the kingdom of God with Him. He wasn't cordial with the neighbors around Him, He wasn't fair or just polite. Jesus was involved, engaged and generous from start to finish. Each one of the lives He touched felt like they were the reason He was there and they mattered—not like they were an interruption. And they mattered just as they were—not as they should be.

Jesus saw the needs of others around Him and stopped and did whatever he could to help them. Jesus prayed, shared the Word of God, brought hope, forgiveness, healing and even food to fill those who reached out. He wasn't afraid of the needs. He asks a blind man in Luke 18:41 (NIV), "What do you want Me to do for you?"

In this life so many are loaded down with heavy burdens it can seem overwhelming at times. We close our eyes to any needs that feel beyond our ability to fill in own strength. Yet to truly follow Jesus, He is asking from us what we do not have the capability in ourselves to give to others in need around us—the kingdom of God.

Matthew 10:5-10 (MSG) says, "Jesus sent his twelve harvest hands out with this charge:

> "Don't begin by traveling to some far-off place to convert unbelievers. And don't try to be dramatic by tackling some public enemy. Go to the lost, confused people right here in the neighborhood. Tell them that the kingdom is here. Bring health to the sick. Raise the dead. Touch the untouchables. Kick out the demons. You have been treated generously, so live generously.
>
> Don't think you have to put on a fund-raising campaign before you start. You don't need a lot of equipment. You are the equipment, and all you need to keep that going is three meals a day. Travel light."

Raise Your Hand

When we share God's heart and purposes, we bring the kingdom where ever we go. As Christ's body, we are the answer to the brokenness in the world. We are His hands and feet to move into the neighborhood, get engaged and let people know they matter.

We are His messengers to compel people to understand they don't have to pretend or be someone for us to accept or receive them. They can come as they are and find a God behind it all that gives all His children unconditional love.

This is the heart of God. As we love Him and walk with Him, more and more our hearts share the passion of His heart. We don't need special education or equipment to be His servants. Sometimes people can think they need special skills in ministry to share the kingdom love with others.

What we need to be willing to do is lay down our own lives and agenda for His. God asks us to care about His purposes coming forth on the earth. This includes people coming to know Him as well as the transformation of His people into greater Christ-likeness—even to the extent of being willing to suffer personal loss, pain, and discomfort to see His purposes come forth.

Rather than choosing to live for our own wealth, comfort, success, or honor, God asks us to live for something much deeper—to live for Him. Ultimately God is calling us to come out and play. He wants us to enter the adventure of a lifetime, sharing His heart for His purposes. And it is out of love for Him we willingly lay down our lives and enter His purposes.

He doesn't just want our leftovers at the end of the day after living for ourselves all day. We hurriedly rush around building our own kingdom that is based on our own purposes. Then we come to Him tired and exhausted wanting Him to refill us and give us strength to live another day like He does not matter much.

We think He is there for when we need Him to bless us or get us out of trouble. What He is really asking for is *all* of us. He wants our days, hours and weeks. He wants to make our priorities. He wants us to live for His purposes and not our own.

He asks us to love Him with all our time and resources, not just when it is convenient, pleasant, affordable or easy. When we are focused on managing our circumstances so that we feel comfortable and safe, we are idolizing comfort over genuinely worshipping God. It is not our circumstances are the source of our joy. What matters is if we love Him with all our heart, all our soul, all our strength, and mind.

He asks us to be committed in our love, not contending or complaining about everything that is not the way we expected. We need to trust that He has a bigger plan and purpose. When we love Him with all our hearts, it is a joy to willingly sacrifice anything that stands in the way—including our pride, reputation and fears.

He asks us to identify with His purposes in other people rather than our own purposes. Instead of looking at how we can benefit from others, God's heart is how we can contribute to them. God is worthy of our all! And in our worship of Him with all that we are and all that we have, we will find deep meaning, significance and purpose for our lives.

Just as the boy who humbly offered the disciples all he had in a few small barley loaves and fish in the story of Jesus feeding 5,000, we humbly offer Jesus what little we have to give in our lives. As we offer it up before Him, He breaks it and makes it more than enough for everyone before us in need. The story is not just about us, it is about Jesus.

God can use what we have in powerful ways when we don't stand in the way and make it about us. We are like the little boy who is humbly willing to give what we have before God. The story is not ultimately about the little boy or his lunch of fish and loaves; the story is about Jesus and how He uses humble and broken people to bring His kingdom in powerful ways to a world that is in desperate need.

Hang Out with the Holy Spirit

Jude speaks about shepherds who are responsible to feed others in the last days and feed only themselves. Jude 1:16 (NIV) says, "These people are grumblers and faultfinders; they follow their own evil desires; they boast about themselves and flatter others for their own advantage."

Jude goes on to say how to avoid becoming a grumbler and faultfinder that feeds only themselves. In Jude 20-21 (NIV) he says, "But you, dear friends, by building yourselves up in your most holy faith and praying in the Holy Spirit, keep yourselves in God's love as you wait for the mercy of our Lord Jesus Christ to bring you to eternal life."

We cannot walk with God and at the same time walk with the world. When our hearts are after what the world offers, we move in the opposite direction of God.

James confronts the church for worldliness in James 4:1-4 (NIV) when he says to them, "What causes fights and quarrels among you? Don't they come from your desires that battle within you? You desire but do not have, so you kill. You covet but you cannot get what you want, so you quarrel and fight. You do not have because you do not ask God. When you ask, you do not receive, because you ask with wrong motives, that you may spend what you get on your pleasures. You adulterous people, don't you know that friendship with the world means enmity against God? Therefore, anyone who chooses to be a friend of the world becomes an enemy of God."

Paul says to the Galatians in Galatians 5:16 (NIV), "So I say, walk by the Spirit, and you will not gratify the desires of the flesh."

When we walk and talk with God, letting the Spirit of God lead in our lives, we will let go of other desires. We cannot live by our sinful nature and also be walking with the Spirit of God.

The Word of God says it is a choice who our hearts will serve. In 1 Kings 18:21 (NIV) "Elijah went before the people and said, 'How long will you waver between two opinions? If the Lord is God, follow Him; but if Baal is God, follow him.' But the people said nothing."

And in Joshua 24:15 (NASB), Joshua said to the people, "If it is disagreeable in your sight to serve the Lord, choose for yourselves today whom you will serve: whether the gods which your fathers served which were beyond the River, or the gods of the Amorites in whose land you are living; but as for me and my house, we will serve the Lord."

Paul easily made this choice as his eyes gazed upon Jesus. He wrote in Philippians 3:7-8 (NASB), "But whatever things were gain to me, those things I have counted as loss for the sake of Christ. More than that, I count all things to be loss in view of the surpassing value of knowing Christ Jesus my Lord, for whom I have suffered the loss of all things, and count them but rubbish so that I may gain Christ."

Paul kept his eyes on his destination. In Philippians 3:10-12 (NASB) he says, "that I may know Him and the power of His resurrection and the fellowship of His sufferings, being conformed to His death; in order that I may attain to the resurrection from the dead. Not that I have already obtained it or have already become perfect, but I press on so that I may lay hold of that for which also I was laid hold of by Christ Jesus."

Paul realized that what was earthly was fleeting and that he had an eternal destination. He said in verse 20-21 (NASB), "For our citizenship is in heaven, from which also we eagerly wait for a Savior, the Lord Jesus Christ; who will transform the body of our humble state into conformity with the body of His glory, by the exertion of the power that He has even to subject all things to Himself."

Coming back to Jude, as our eyes stay fixed on Jesus, it is Him that enables us to live according to the Spirit. Jude 1:24 (NIV) says, "To Him who is able to keep you from stumbling and to present you before His glorious presence without fault and with great joy—to the only God our Savior be glory, majesty, power and authority, through Jesus Christ our Lord, before all ages, now and forevermore! Amen."

As we spend time walking with God and living according to the Spirit, we are filled with His power to fulfill His purposes. He directs our path and gives us what we need for the moment. We not only survive, but thrive in our days as His purposes are fulfilled through us. He is our ever-present help moment by moment. But first we must slow down and listen.

Stop and Think

Sometimes we just need to pause and think about our lives—*Selah.* We need to slow down and listen to what our hearts are speaking. Take the time to listen rather than hurriedly going through our days at a high speed. We need to reflect on the circumstances in our lives and ask for what God's invitation is amid what we are experiencing.

Reflection is necessary in our lives to grow. We need to listen and learn from our experiences. When David wrote a Psalm, he often had a pause in it. Selah. It was a time to stop and think about what was being said. What does it mean to us? What is God speaking in it? How do we see God more clearly through it? In pausing, one could connect in that place of deep calling onto deep.

In taking the time to pause, we reorient ourselves to God and to others. Too often in our busy society we push from one thing to another. We have hurry sickness. We rush through everything just to find more to do on the other side. We lack time for rest and reflection. Because of this, our connection to God is superficial. Our only time to process is as we sleep, which results in even this being shallow and poor quality. Thus, our lives miss an important point—purpose.

It isn't until we slow down and listen that we can connect with the bigger purpose God has for us. Our lives take on meaning only as we come present to God. In slowing down, we become more effective. Our moves become acts of God's wisdom by His Spirit rather than frantic flailing around in our efforts to accomplish the next thing on our list.

As we spend time listening for God, we will become increasingly more led by the Spirit. The Spirit will lead and guide us. He will fill us and give us revelation of Jesus. He will open up His Word to us and convict us of sin. He will also strengthen us against difficulty and temptation.

As the gentle Dove of the Spirit came to rest on Jesus when He came up from His baptism, the Spirit of God rests on us and gives us a sense of peace to go through our day as we slow down and center ourselves upon Jesus. We enter the flow of being led by His Spirit. When our hearts are open, our hands open too. We are in a position of surrender to God in meekness rather than plowing ahead and making things happen by our own strength.

We become like a child and are willing to yield to the plan of our Father. We run to God as a child who seeks his Father's protection and care. We were created to be loved and give that love away to others. A sense of self-importance and self-reliance give way to the simplicity of a trusting open heart in childlikeness.

This was the heart of David—a man after God's own heart. It was opposite of the religious folks. It is possible to be Christian but dwell far from God and not know the nearness of His intimate presence or be formed more and more into His likeness.

Many Christians go to church on Sunday but stand far off from Him on the sidelines. They are Christians by the world standards but their hearts are not truly pursuing Him. They do not know the daily nearness of His presence.

Ultimately if we are pursuing Christ with all our hearts, we will take on His character. It is our nearness to Him that forms us to be like Him. However, in this place of nearness to Him, we still all look and minister very differently from each other as Christians. How our witness looks will be different based upon how we are individually wired.

For example, John the Baptist came out of the desert baptizing and calling people to repent. He was a prophet whose purpose was to prepare the way in the hearts of men for the Lord's coming by calling people to repent and baptizing them.

Matthew 3:4 (AMP) says about him, "This same John's garments were made of camel's hair, and he wore a leather girdle about his waist; and his food was locusts and wild honey." Both his dress and his demeanor were consistent with who he was, his calling, and how he was specifically wired.

Matthew, on the other hand, was wired totally different that John the Baptist. He was a tax collector who was called to follow Jesus. He was someone who was received by other tax collectors and sinners. As Matthew invited Jesus to his home, "many tax collectors and [especially wicked] sinners" came over and sat with them and the disciples (Matthew 9:10, AMP).

Not a great deal is known about Matthew other than he was one of the twelve disciples. He was literate, knew the books of the Old Testament, and was at least somewhat educated. What is known is that a significant part of his witness was writing the first gospel.

Knowing the importance of lineage to his fellow Israelites, Matthew starts the gospel by first establishing the lineage of Jesus as the Messiah. Matthew also draws special attention to the three sets of fourteen generations.

He writes in Matthew 1:17 (AMP), "So all the generations from Abraham to David are fourteen, from David to the Babylonian exile (deportation) fourteen generations, from the Babylonian exile to the Christ fourteen generations."

Another witness who was very different than both John the Baptist and Matthew was the woman at the well. She had gone to the well to draw water when she ran into Jesus. She was a Samaritan woman who had five prior husbands and was living with another man who was not her husband (John 4:18).

Jesus didn't judge her but had offered her living water to drink. He treated her with care and respect. She was the first person to whom Jesus revealed Himself as Messiah that all were waiting for in the Gospel of John. After hearing the good news, she left her water at the well and ran and told everyone that she met a man who told her everything she ever did and asked, "Can this be [is not this] the Christ?" (John 4:29, AMP).

John 4:39 (AMP) goes on to say, "Now numerous Samaritans from that town believed in and trusted in Him because of what the woman said when she declared and testified, He told me everything that I ever did."

Another witness that was different than these was the paralyzed man. Jesus told him in Matthew 9:2 (AMP), "Take courage, son; your sins are forgiven and the penalty remitted." Then knowing the people's hearts did not believe He could forgive sins, He went on to make him a witness of His forgiveness through this man's healing.

In Matthew 9:5 (AMP) Jesus asks, "For which is easier: to say, Your sins are forgiven and the penalty remitted, or to say, Get up and walk? But in order that you may know that the Son of Man has authority on earth to forgive sins and remit the penalty, He then said to the paralyzed man, Get up! Pick up your sleeping pad and go to your own house."

The paralyzed man was not specifically witnessing Christ, but by stepping into what God had for him by faith, he was a witness to all around him of God's goodness. Matthew 9:8 (AMP) says, "When the crowds saw it, they were struck with fear and awe; and they recognized God and praised and thanked Him, Who had given such power and authority to men."

Other examples of witnesses are the two blind men that Jesus healed. They cried out for Jesus to have pity and mercy on them (Matthew 9:27). He opened their eyes and healed them, then charged them not to let anyone know. Matthew 9:31 (AMP) says, "But they went off and blazed and spread His fame abroad throughout that whole district."

Lastly, the Roman centurion (captain) was an example of another witness shining the light of Christ by being who God wired Him to be (Matthew 8:5). He came to Jesus begging Him for help. The Roman soldiers were viewed by the Israelites as ruthless authorities. Yet, this centurion came to Jesus humbly begging Him to heal his servant boy who was back lying in his house distressed and with intense pain.

This young servant boy was a slave who was not capable to work. A slave who could not work for his keep would most likely be discarded. Yet this centurion had a heart that was full of compassion. He put value on this slave and became his servant as he cared for all this slave's needs.

This centurion, who would have been hated by the Israelites for who he was, not only showed compassion and mercy towards a paralyzed slave that most Israelites lacked, but he also demonstrated tremendous faith. He did not feel worthy to have Jesus to his house, and believed if Jesus spoke a word, that the servant would be healed.

Matthew 8:10 (AMP) says, "When Jesus heard him, He marveled and said to those who followed Him [who adhered steadfastly to Him, conforming to His example in living and, if need be, in dying also], I tell you truly, I have not found so much faith as this with anyone, even in Israel."

Play Dress Up

We have heard it said that as Christians we need to be a good witness to those who do not know Christ. Sometimes in this, we may think if we say the right things and look like we have everything together that others will want to be Christians. And if we don't put on a good front, it will be a hindrance to them. However, trying to put on an image to get others to do what we want, even if it is for their benefit, is manipulation.

What matters is not our external appearances or specific actions alone; what matters is our heart towards God and the corresponding heart towards others.

The witness that we present is based upon who we are at the core and our genuine exuberance for God. It is our passion that shines through—not getting our external actions, behaviors and dress just right.

A friend of mine recently told me a story about a beautiful young woman in college. In class when people would mention God in a wrong light, she couldn't help herself to speak up. She would tell the person in her class with passion, "God is not like that, He loves you!"

For someone else who is wired differently, this may be totally inappropriate, appear phony and be out of character. Their means of being a witness may be noticing the person in the class who never talks with anyone else, always looks down and appears lonely. This person may have compassion for them being left out and make friends. By their genuine friendship, they become a witness to their friends of His goodness. And by their genuine friendship eventually lead them to know the Lord.

This was the same for the disciples. They all were wired differently and demonstrated their witness uniquely. Peter was boisterous, loved the limelight and was outspoken. When the Holy Spirit was poured out at Pentecost, Peter rose up filled with the Spirit and witnessed Christ to the devout Jews from every country. Because of his witness that day, about 3000 people came to know Christ (Acts 2).

Andrew, Peter's brother, on the other hand, was wired totally different. We do not read any stories of him giving major speeches or leading thousands to Christ like his brother. However, Andrew was not without significant influence. His influence seemed to be more on an individual level. It was because of Andrew that Peter came to know the Lord.

While the disciples were wired differently from each other, Jesus sent them all out to bring the kingdom of God to those around them who needed it. All of them were counted on by Jesus to bring the Gospel. They were not to go to a people in a far-away land that they did not know, but to the people in their very backyard.

Jesus tells them in Matthew 10:5-6 (AMP), "Do not go among the Gentiles, and do not go into a city of the Samaritans; but rather go to the lost sheep of the house of Israel." They were not to take anything with them but use what was put right in front of them. And they were not only to be witnesses, but to bring the kingdom of God to those who needed it with demonstration of its power.

As Jesus endued them with His power and authority, He instructed them in Matthew 10:7-8 (AMP), "And as you go, preach, saying, 'The kingdom of heaven is at hand.' Heal the sick, raise the dead, cleanse the lepers, cast out demons. Freely you have received, freely give."

All Christians are called to be witnesses of Christ. Jesus says we are not only the light to the world but the salt of the earth that makes others thirsty for the kingdom (Matthew 5:19).

And while each person is wired uniquely and their witness looks very different from other Christians, followers of Christ do have common characteristics in their witness with each other. Foremost, Christians are called to love God with all their heart and love others as themselves.

Jesus spoke in Matthew 22:37-38 (AMP), "You shall love the Lord your God with all your heart and with all your soul and with all your mind (intellect). This is the great (primary, most important, principal) and first commandment. And a second is like it: You shall love your neighbor as [you do] yourself."

Do Your Best

A key characteristic that connects all Christians beyond brokenness and a deep love for Christ and others is passion.

These Christians stepped beyond the sidelines, found their passion and stepped into it with the purpose of glorifying God and doing His will.

Jesus, while He was on the earth, was incredibly passionate. Because of this, He was willing to endure anything to pursue His passion—people no longer being separated from God.

If we really want to make a difference, we cannot live half-heartedly. We need to bring our best to the game every day. We need to look differently than the world and not fit into the crowds of people around us.

Sometimes we can think it is humility to look, act and fit in with everyone else around us. It really is hiding. We are burying our treasure, the gifts we have been given, rather than using and investing them in the world around us.

In connecting with our passion, we are looking at what gets us fired up. What do we get so angry about that we feel it deep down in our gut? Where do we rejoice and find our greatest joy? What makes us absolutely elated? What do we dream about and what does that dream tell us about who we are, how we are wired and what we love?

Often our dreams can be way further down the road so we may shove them aside as unrealistic. But they tell us something about where our heart wants to go. An old saying applies, "By the yard it's hard but by the inch it is a cinch."

Following your passions does not mean you need to drop everything in your life and go in a different direction that seems irresponsible. We start putting our hands to our passions in little ways right where we are at. We start clearing room for our passion by getting rid of some of the clutter in our lives.

For example, I am passionate about justice for children. I believe all children should be safe, cared for, given opportunities and protected from predators. When I hear talks from justice organizations who are protecting kids, I get emotional about it. When children are being mistreated, I feel it physically in my gut.

However, even though I am passionate about children being cared for, I don't believe God has for me to leave everything in my life and all the people I am responsible for to join in the work they are doing and go to another country to help. At the same time, I have found some ways to move towards and pursue my passion in this area.

As I put my hands toward helping and serving in pursuit of my passion in this area, as prompted by my heart, I find it grows. I have become more passionate about justice for children over time.

When we move towards our passions, they grow. If we are feeling apathetic in our faith journey, it may be that we are caught in the day-to-day routines and we are not allowing ourselves to press toward what we have passion about. In the same way that passions grow as we move towards them, they languish when we move away from them.

Love is a verb. It is an action rather than just a feeling. Feelings are inconsistent and will languish over time. However, those things that we have put into action become part of who we are becoming. Getting some time away and thinking about what is important to us and the direction we want to head is imperative in going a way that will be fulfilling.

It is in the place before God that we can weed out our desires from our passions. We may desire a bigger home, more money, and a greater position. But in pursuing these, we will find that in the end they are empty.

Like Jesus who gave His life for us to have salvation and no longer be distant from God, our passions involve laying down our lives for others. It is not an easy road that will only be about us. Our passions draw us toward a greater purpose of love of others.

God-given passions are sacrificial rather than self-serving. They will also draw us closer to God as they require more than what we have available to give within ourselves.

When we allow everything else to clutter up our hearts and choke our passions out, we will never go beyond half-hearted efforts that involve no cost or sacrifice to ourselves. We will find that our lives feel unfulfilled and like something is missing.

The 'something' that is missing is not obtaining more, having more, or buying more. This only further clutters our heart up and chokes out our passion. The something that is missing is our sacrificial love. We are only fulfilled when we are giving ourselves away for others. When we are an on-ramp for someone else, our lives take on new meaning and significance.

John the Baptist had tremendous passion around preparing the way for Jesus to come forth. He put his whole heart and efforts into pursuing this path. As he was following his passion, he found significance. He was making an incredible difference. As Jesus came and started to draw the people away from John, John the Baptist told others, "He must become greater, I must become less" (John 3:30).

Ultimately, where his passion for making a way for Jesus led John was to a place of losing himself completely in it. He lost his life to beheading. He was willing to die for his passion of making the way for Jesus.

Lord, we are new creations, created in You to do good works. You have wired each one of us uniquely to serve Your purposes. Connect our hearts to Your purposes and send us out to serve Your kingdom.

Ready, Set, Go!

It is only in exercising our faith and stepping out in our areas of passion that we have a significant impact. What does it look like to have robust faith? How does living the adventure look for us?

John the Baptist not only had passion, but he had tremendous faith and was willing to enter the adventure that Jesus had for Him in preparing the way for Him. It was once he stepped out in faith that his passion made a difference. He courageously bounded out into the adventure that God called him into with unbridled passion for the purpose of seeing the kingdom of God come forth.

Sometimes we go through the motions of our daily routines and responsibilities, but fail to really look to God to lead and guide us. We give God a tip of the hat by reading our Bible for a few minutes and listening to some worship music but then we go on with our day without further acknowledging Him. Our days become routine and we carry God around more like a sentimental ragdoll that we pull out when we need some comfort.

We may hear an invitation to a greater adventure at times but we drown it out with the million other things we have on our list to complete. Or we hesitate and debate until we can find enough excuses not to step out and to go back to our routine.

Financially, most of us in America have all our basic needs met, so it is easy to rely on our own strength rather than depend upon God. Once we run into trouble and difficulty, then we look to Him for answers.

Are we really living a God-led adventure by faith? Are we thriving and flourishing? Or do we feel more like we are surviving day-to-day?

Joshua was someone who lived the adventure by faith. In Joshua 1:1-9 (MSG), God encouraged Joshua to step up into the calling He had for him and enter the adventure. God told Joshua,

> "Get going. Cross this Jordan River, you and all the people. Cross to the country I'm giving to the People of Israel. I'm giving you every square inch of the land you set your foot on—just as I promised Moses. It's all yours.
>
> All your life, no one will be able to hold out against you. In the same way I was with Moses, I'll be with you. I won't give up on you; I won't leave you. Strength! Courage! You are going to lead this people

> to inherit the land that I promised to give their ancestors.
>
> Give it everything you have, heart and soul. Make sure you carry out The Revelation that Moses commanded you, every bit of it. Don't get off track, either left or right, so as to make sure you get to where you're going.
>
> And don't for a minute let this Book of The Revelation be out of mind. Ponder and meditate on it day and night, making sure you practice everything written in it. Then you'll get where you're going; then you'll succeed.
>
> Haven't I commanded you? Strength! Courage! Don't be timid; don't get discouraged. God, your God, is with you every step you take."

The people of God were about to take a journey into the land that had been promised to them. Under the leadership of Joshua, they would cross the Jordan and take the land from people who were fierce giants, with huge and well-fortified cities (Numbers 13:28). The people of God were like grasshoppers in their sight (Numbers 13:33).

When the previous generation of Israelites had heard about the people who lived in the land, they shrunk back in fear. They even threatened to stone Moses and Aaron. And after this initial response of quaking in fear, they then tried to possess the land by their own strength. They went up against the Amalekites and Canaanites who lived in the hill country and were totally defeated. They did not have the power in their own strength to take the land.

Having learned from the mistakes of the earlier generation, this new generation of Israelites would cross over the Jordan and take the land in faith and obedience. Rather than focusing on the enemy and their own ability to take the land, this generation had their eyes on God—His strength and power to achieve His promises. And they had willing hearts to follow God into all that He had for them.

Psalm 84:5-7 (NIV) says, "Blessed are those whose strength is in You, who have set their hearts on pilgrimage. As they pass through the Valley of Baca, they make it a place of springs; the autumn rains also cover it with pools. They go from strength to strength, till each appears before God in Zion."

The Reubenintes, Gadites, and half-tribe of Manasseh told Joshua, "Everything you commanded us, we'll do. Wherever you send us, we'll go. We obeyed Moses to the letter; we'll also obey you—we just pray that God, your God, will be with you as he was with Moses. Anyone who questions what you say and refuses to obey whatever you command him will be put to death. Strength! Courage!" (Joshua 1:16-18, MSG)

Double Dared

Moses confronted the temptation to fear, preparing this generation for what was ahead. He told them, "When you go to war against your enemy and see horses and chariots and soldiers far outnumbering you, do not recoil in fear of them; God, your God, who brought you up out of Egypt is with you. When the battle is about to begin, let the priest come forward and speak to the troops. He'll say, 'Attention, Israel. In a few minutes you're going to do battle with your enemies. Don't waver in resolve. Don't fear. Don't hesitate. Don't panic. God, your God, is right there with you, fighting with you against your enemies, fighting to win'" (Deuteronomy 20:1-4, MSG).

There was also an invitation for the people of God to display courage and exercise their faith. As they followed Moses and now Joshua, they clearly saw this kind of gutsy leadership demonstrated. And people more naturally follow what they see their leaders do over what they are told to do by their leaders.

We do courageous acts despite our fears and insecurities. It is never easy to step into them and always involves sacrificing our comfortability. Acting courageously takes a commitment to something greater that pushes us beyond our fears and gives us a willingness and resolve to press forward despite voices of fear and doubt still screeching in our ears.

Sometimes courageous acts are done with little forethought because the moment calls for it. Other times it is having preparation that helps one move forward courageously. The more times we are courageous, the easier it gets to say yes to the invitation.

Courage is something we need to exercise. Just like using certain muscles, as we put it into action repeatedly, it becomes easier each time. As we step out in faith in small things as we are going along our regular ordinary days, we exercise courage and it grows. Exercising our courage helps to prepare us for the times we really need it.

When David went against Goliath, he was courageous. Everyone else was terrified of Goliath and it immobilized them. But as others cowered, David asked, "What's in it for the man who kills that Philistine and gets rid of this ugly blot on Israel's honor? Who does he think he is, anyway, this uncircumcised Philistine, taunting the armies of God-Alive?" (1 Samuel 17:26, MSG)

David explains where his courage came from in 1 Samuel 17:34-37 (MSG) when he tells Saul, "I've been a shepherd, tending sheep for my father. Whenever a lion or bear came and took a lamb from the flock, I'd go after it, knock it down, and rescue the lamb. If it turned on me, I'd grab it by the throat, wring its neck, and kill it. Lion or bear, it made no difference—I killed it. And I'll do the same to this Philistine pig who is taunting the troops of God-Alive. God, who delivered me from the teeth of the lion and the claws of the bear, will deliver me from this Philistine."

David was faithful in the small things he encountered day-to-day which built his courage to step forward in faith when it really counted. He did not sit back in comfort, ease and complacency. He was actively engaged in the purposes of God in the middle of the mundane of life. No matter how little or insignificant the small act of obedience seemed, David stepped forward in faithfulness and faith.

As David exercised his faith, he learned that God strengthened him to accomplish all that He asked of him.

A quote from Mother Teresa declares, "Be faithful in small things because it is in them that your strength lies."

Playing The "Yes, And" Game

As we are faithful in the small things, our faith grows. We need to take advantage of these little opportunities that come our way.

Ecclesiastes 9:9 (MSG) says, "Whatever turns up, grab it and do it. And heartily! This is your last and only chance at it."

We live in the land of opportunities so we can think our opportunities to death. We don't do something because it does not seem to be a good time. We tell ourselves that we need to wait for a better time when we are more prepared. We count costs as if we had a million chances and miss opportunities.

As we practice doubt, over analysis and saying no to opportunities that may be over our heads, it becomes a greater stronghold of our lives. Many people are just not willing to step up and take a risk as they fear the cost or don't want to be inconvenienced.

We are also bombarded with media reasons not to do something for someone else. We hear the news stories of how someone stopped to help someone on the side of the road and they were harmed. It was some sort of a scam. Or how someone tried to help, failed and was then later sued for it. We then pass by an opportunity to help even though we felt a tug on our heart. While we have to exercise some precaution, we sometimes pass by and *leave it for someone else* because of fear or busyness.

Statistics show that we are much more likely to overlook someone on the side of the road who needs help when there are others who are also on the road who could stop. However, if we are in a deserted location where there are not others around who could stop to help, we are more likely to stop and help even though we may feel inconvenienced.

Hebrews 13:12 (NIV) says, "Do not forget to show hospitality to strangers, for by so doing some people have shown hospitality to angels without knowing it."

We may become encouragers of other people who are fulfilling God's calling rather than fulfilling our own calling. While it is great to speak life and encourage others, sometimes we can become more a fan than a player. We feel engaged by cheering others on but think of them as different than us. Instead of getting off the bench and playing our part, we look to others to make the plays. We do not trust that God has a position for us to play so we act as sideliners. We all have gifts to bring to the table and a part to play.

When what God has for us does not feel comfortable, safe and secure, we can be reluctant to move towards it. It is so easy to make excuses for why it isn't a good time, the conditions are not right yet, or we are not sure we are really,

I mean really, hearing from God. Plus, who wants to make decisions that look a little crazy when we cannot logically justify them other than, "I felt God told me." We can have such reluctant hearts.

We also weigh if we think we can do it well in our own strength. If we can't do it in our own strength, we pass up the opportunity. Like in the case of Joshua and the people, God was inviting them into something over their heads. It was in their weakness they would see God come through in power. It was in saying 'yes' to God, not one's own abilities, that the adventure began.

What would it look like to take on a practice of saying 'yes' to what comes our way when it is over our heads and we feel prompted? Whatever turns up that connects with our hearts, to say yes and do it heartily, like it was the last chance we would ever have? What would it look like to trust God to meet us in it and supply what is needed?

In the same way that as we exercise courage and it grows, if we act on our fears, they will continue to grow and become a stronghold in our lives. 1 John 4:18 notes that fear has to do with punishment. In some translations, it says where there is fear, there is torment. Where one is in fear, they anticipate negative and harmful consequences for their actions. As one continues to act on their fears, the fears grow stronger.

We find the strength to resist fear by growing in intimacy with God. 1 John 4:18 (NKJV) says, "There is no fear in love, but perfect love casts out fear."

Perfect love casts out fear because we can trust in the goodness of the One who loves us—God. When we can trust in and rely on the love of God for us, we become free to act accordingly.

Joshua and others who demonstrated courage did so out of a heart of intimacy with God. They spent time in God's presence, knowing Him and learning to trust Him. It was that intimate relationship with God that gave them courage.

Jesus and the disciples who followed him stood in the middle of tremendous difficulties with great faith and courage because they had a deeper yes in their hearts. It is for that deeper yes to Jesus that they were willing to walk forward into incredibly fearful situations.

Like David, Joshua fully relied on the love of God and lived his life out of this place of intimacy. It was God who gave both of them the strength and courage to step forward and follow. In knowing deeply that they could depend on God for anything and He was faithful to come through, they could trust in the most difficult situations. And even if they failed, they knew God would be with them through it. Even death did not ultimately deter them because they knew and trusted God's love. They had tasted deeply of it.

However, without ever saying yes, we cannot learn to trust God for what we need. Until we say yes to a few things that are over our heads, how will we ever know His faithfulness to meet us in these places? It takes starting to say yes for us to grow in trust that God will see us through every challenge He calls us into.

Pinky Swear

As God takes us into His purposes for us, He does not want us to obtain our worth or find our identity in the land He brings us into. Rather He would have us find our worth in Him. It is not 'getting there' that is most important but being on the journey with God. As God nestles us into His love and leads us along the way, He provides all that we need.

Being faithful dealing with trials and difficulties, may result in us being tested by success. Success can sometimes throw us off course more so than failure or difficulties. This happened to the Israelites as they had their first great victory with Jericho. After their first success, some of the people were unfaithful regarding the things that were devoted to destruction (Joshua 7:1). They took some of the possessions and hid them. Their success in battle resulted in them attributing it to their own abilities and feeling entitled to take some of the gain.

They also became overconfident in their abilities. After spying out Ai, the men said to Joshua, "Not all the army will have to go up against Ai. Send two or three thousand men to take it and do not weary the whole army, for only a few people live there" (Joshua 7:3, NIV). To their surprise, the army was routed by the men of Ai and struck down on the slopes (Joshua 7:5).

When Joshua cried out to the Lord about it, the Lord told them that they were defeated because they had lied and stolen, and this was why they could not stand against their enemies (Joshua 7:11-12). Proverbs 25:28 (NASB) says, "Like a city that is broken into and without walls is a man who has no control over his spirit."

We cannot expect to stand strong in faith and courage when our lives lack character. Jesus says in Mark 3:25 (NIV), "If a house is divided against itself, that house cannot stand."

We need to keep God as first in our hearts and our deepest motivation to love Him with all our heart, mind and soul. Bringing Him glory and loving Him with our whole hearts needs to be our ultimate motive in doing good. If our success, image, status or position in comparison to others motivate us, we will be led off course by it.

When David met challenges and difficulties, he chose faithfulness to God over the kingship God was giving Him. He refused to seek after or grasp to be king. He saw the treasure, not as kingship, but in his relationship with God. Because of this, David was free to worship God through his God-given purpose rather than strive and manipulate to attain or maintain what God had given him.

This is totally opposite of Saul. Because being king was more important to Saul than his relationship with God, he lacked the confidence needed to live out the purposes God had for him in it. He was filled with fear that someone would take over his position. Since he couldn't trust God, constant anxiety caused him great affliction. It also drove him to make horrible choices in slaughtering others who he saw as a potential threat.

When we enter into our calling, there is a risk we will take credit for getting ourselves there and become proud. Moses warns the people in Deuteronomy 8:17-18 (MSG) about thinking they obtained their purpose in life by their own might. He tells them, "If you start thinking to yourselves, 'I did all this. And all by myself. I'm rich. It's all mine!'—well, think again. Remember that God, your God, gave you the strength to produce all this wealth so as to confirm the covenant that he promised to your ancestors—as it is today."

When we strive after our purposes, we are making it about the destination itself rather than about the relationship with the one who gives us purpose. In entering the promises of God, there is the risk that we will seek fulfillment of the promise to satisfy our thirst rather than fulfillment by the God who has been with us along the whole journey.

Moses warns against this in Deuteronomy 8:11-16 (MSG):

> "Make sure you don't forget God, your God, by not keeping his commandments, his rules and regulations that I command you today. Make sure that when you eat and are satisfied, build pleasant houses and settle in, see your herds and flocks flourish and more and more money come in, watch your standard of living going up and up—make sure you don't become so full of yourself and your things that you forget God, your God, the God who delivered you from Egyptian slavery; the God who

> led you through that huge and fearsome wilderness, those desolate, arid badlands crawling with fiery snakes and scorpions; the God who gave you water gushing from hard rock; the God who gave you manna to eat in the wilderness, something your ancestors had never heard of, in order to give you a taste of the hard life, to test you so that you would be prepared to live well in the days ahead of you."

Our purposes and the positions we are given in life, when fulfilled in honor of God, will bring life to others as well as ourselves. We will both flourish. It will be with a spirit of humility we will complete them knowing we did not get there by ourselves and are not sustained by our own strength.

However, being in God's will does not mean that all will go perfectly. As a student is not above his master, we will at times experience persecution just as Jesus did. When we are doing the will of God and bringing forth kingdom purposes, we will experience opposition to contend with.

Sometimes we expect that if we are doing what God calls us to it will be as easy as walking on water. We forget that Peter sank when Jesus called him out. Just like the Israelites, we will have difficulties to face and overcome.

At times, we will sink and need Jesus to rescue us. In fulfilling the purposes of God, we can feel in over our heads when we fail. But, we are never outside of the reach of God to pull us up and sustain us. Even when we fail, we keep rising back up and pressing forward, saying yes to God's leading.

We will also have a sense of joy and rest as we possess the land God calls us to (Joshua 22:4). We know it is what we were made for and God brought us into it and will sustain us in it. Ultimately, it is not about reaching a destiny but our relationship with God along the way. As we hold onto the hand of our Father and trust Him to help us, our journey will be filled with wonder, awe and joy.

When we are no longer stepping out or saying yes to the adventure God has set before us, our lives can easily sink into being comfortable. In this place, we stop exercising faith and courage. We go through the motions and are not fully engaged in the present moment.

We may not even realize it when we are in a place of comfortability and have stopped taking risks. We keep going along doing the same things as in the past but feel like something is missing and our lives lack some luster. We are no longer attentive to invitations, no longer saying yes to the next thing and fully embracing the opportunities before us. We may even stop going out of our way to be faithful in the small things.

Fear or discouragement can also keep us from staying engaged and living the adventure God has for us. Fear can immobilize us if we let it. Or, being discouraged, we may feel like a failure and incapable of success. We lose hope. Something happens in our life where we struggle so we start playing it safe.

When we pass by opportunities to exercise courage and faith, we are practicing something else instead. Whatever we do over and over, becomes habit. As we practice pushing off God's nudge and acting out on our own will, it becomes easier to no to God's nudge in the future.

What we need to realize is failing to do the good we know we should do and have been nudged to do is just as much sin as acting in a hurtful or harmful way. James 4:17 (NIV) says, "If anyone, then, knows the good they ought to do and doesn't do it, it is sin for them."

By failing to do the good we know we should do, we are failing to do His will in the world. We are withholding good and burying our talents. We are not trusting in His goodness and love for us or truly resting in our relationship with Him.

At the same time, resting in our relationship with Him does not mean striving or working hard at getting everything right. It is not by self-efforts or striving that we will please God. Rather, we enter into what God has for us in the moment by faith and obedience.

Hebrews 11:6 says that without faith it is impossible to please God. As we trust His goodness and His love for us, we are free to obey God from the heart rather than through legalistic works of striving.

Entering into the promises of God for our lives requires dependence. When God presents to us a purpose that He has for us beyond our capacity to achieve in our own abilities, we need Him to accomplish it. It is as we step out over our heads and know we cannot do it on our own that we learn to depend upon God.

When we first hear the invitation from Him, there may be a temptation to cower and shrink back in fear in light of our own inadequacies. Another temptation is to try to make it something smaller, more controllable and manageable so we can achieve it in our own strength.

In both cases, we fail to fully enter into the promises of God. We fail to trust Him. He knows how He made us and how to make us fruitful. We need to be willing to say yes because we trust in His love and goodness rather than willful or fearful about our own inadequacies. God is more than capable of bringing us into His purposes in His time.

Simon Says, "Go!"

Gideon is a great example of someone called into something more than he could imagine. An angel appeared to Gideon and told him, "The Eternal One is with you, mighty warrior" (Judges 6:12, VOICE). The angel told him, "Go out with your strength and rescue Israel from the oppression of Midian. Do you understand that I am the one sending you?" (Judges 6:14, VOICE)

Gideon could not believe that God was really sending him. He responded, "But, Lord, how am I supposed to deliver Israel? My family is the weakest in the tribe of Manasseh, and I am the least of my family" (Judges 6:15, VOICE).

Eventually after testing God more than once, Gideon believed and obeyed. He called the tribes of Israel to fight with him and they gathered and followed him. God provided more than enough warriors. He then even had Gideon reduce the number of warriors to fight from 32,000 to 300. With this little troop, Gideon led the people to victory.

God calls us to live differently than the world around us. He calls us to be fully engaged and passionate rather than indifferent. When we are going through our days feeling indifferent, our hearts are not connected. We have shut down emotionally to God. We may need to get with God and let Him tenderize our hearts to His purposes.

He calls us to care about what He cares about rather than our own agendas. He desires for us to put His purposes first in our lives. In letting Him lead rather than driving our own agenda, we will find an adventure we could never imagine.

Rather than standing back, we enter the invitations that He puts in front of us. We move from standing on the sidelines to entering the game. As we do, our lives begin to take on new meaning and purpose. We will find we care more and more about the things He cares about. Love is a verb that grows as we put our hands to what our heart prompts.

When it feels over our heads, He calls us to humbly and courageously look at who He is in light of challenges and difficulties rather than our own sufficiency. As we see Him meet us in the hard places and provide what we need, we have opportunities that we never would have otherwise to grow in faith.

But just as it was with the Israelites, it is a choice to open our ears to what God is speaking and choose to listen and follow. We must choose to live courageously and trust God will take care of the outcome as we step out in obedience.

As we follow Him, we learn that it is not about what we can provide or have in resources, but who He is and what He can do. When He promises, He fulfills His promises as we trust in Him and look to Him.

Jesus was bold, passionate, compassionate and humble. As we allow God to make us courageous, we are following Christ and growing in His image. We become more like Him.

Romans 13:4 (NIV) says, "Clothe yourself with the Lord Jesus Christ, and do not think about how to gratify the desires of the sinful nature."

Just as with Gideon, God will use our gifts, passions, and unique wiring to fulfill His calling. And God will use our weaknesses to keep us humble. God formed each one of us in our mother's womb with much forethought about how He created and wired us. Every day was written in His book before one of them came to be. We are just perfect for the calling that He has in mind for us.

David says in Psalm 139:13-16 (NIV), "For You created my inmost being; You knit me together in my mother's womb. I praise You because I am fearfully and wonderfully made; Your works are wonderful, I know that full well. My frame was not hidden from You, when I was made in secret, and skillfully wrought in the depths of the earth; Your eyes have seen my unformed substance; and in Your book were all written the days that were ordained for me, when there was not one of them."

It is when we fully utilize our gifts, passions, values and even weaknesses in line with His purposes that we find a place of contentment. We have rest in our labors with Him because we were made for them. Ultimately, it is not about achieving a certain destiny but the joy in the journey of partnering with God in what He has called us to do. We feel most alive when we fully embrace His will.

Lord, we are so thankful for You. You are the only true Treasure. May our lives be filled with Your passion and moments with You. Open our eyes and hearts to all that You are and all that You have for us— in every day and every moment. Invite us into the adventure and give us hearts that quickly say 'yes.' Let us love You and others around us bravely.

You will find Me in everything,
When you seek Me with all your heart

Seeking
takes on new meaning
    as we grow in faith
Learning
    then living
      then loving

all things teach Christ
beholding you in the moment
in the face of the one before us
In the world around us
In the silence of prayer
In the hope for the children in Africa
In the flickering flame
and in the burning
Finding you are with us
    in everything

Make yourself known
    today in the world
through our hearts and our love

End Notes

Chapter 2: Come Out to Play!

1. The Strong's Exhaustive Concordance. THAYER'S GREEK LEXICON, Electronic Database. Located at: http://biblehub.com/greek/1096.htm. Last Accessed: 10/5/2017.
2. The New Strong's Dictionary of Hebrew and Greek Words. Nashville: Thomas Nelson, 1997, c1996, S. H4161.

Chapter 4: Shine!

3. Strong, James: The Exhaustive Concordance of the Bible: Showing Every Word of the Text of the Common English Version of the Canonical Books, and Every Occurrence of Each Word in Regular Order. electronic ed. Ontario: Woodside Bible Fellowship., 1996, S. G2920
4. Brown, Bene, Ph.D., L.M.S.W., The Gifts of Imperfection: Let Go of Who You Think You're Supposed to Be and Embrace Who You Are. Hazelden. Center City, MN. 2010.
5. Brown, Bene, Ph.D., L.M.S.W., The Gifts of Imperfection: Let Go of Who You Think You're Supposed to Be and Embrace Who You Are. Hazelden. Center City, MN. 2010.
6. The New Strong's Dictionary of Hebrew and Greek Words. Nashville: Thomas Nelson, 1997, c1996, S. H4137.

Chapter 5: Have a Good Attitude!

7. Strong, James: The Exhaustive Concordance of the Bible: Showing Every Word of the Text of the Common English Version of the Canonical Books, and Every Occurrence of Each Word in Regular Order. electronic ed. Ontario: Woodside Bible Fellowship., 1996, S. G3936
8. Thomas Nelson Publishers: Nelson's Quick Reference Topical Bible Index. Nashville, Tenn.: Thomas Nelson Publishers, 1995 (Nelson's Quick Reference), S. 663
9. Vine, W. E. ; Unger, Merrill F. ; White, William: Vine's Complete Expository Dictionary of Old and New Testament Words. Nashville: T. Nelson, 1996, S. 2:73
10. Hayford, Jack W. ; Thomas Nelson Publishers: Hayford's Bible Handbook. Nashville: Thomas Nelson Publishers, 1995

Chapter 6: Dance for Joy!

11. Lloyd-Jones, Sally. Illustrated by Jago. Thoughts That Make Your Heart Sing. Zondervan, Grand Rapids, MI. 2012.
12. Lloyd-Jones, Sally. Illustrated by Jago. The Jesus Storybook Bible. Zondervan, Grand Rapids, MI. 2007.
13. Abhishek Joshi. How did you learn to dance? Best Answer Chosen by 'the chameleon.' Located at: http://answers.yahoo.com/question/index?qid=20071218162023AAufAXS. Last Accessed: 5/31/10

About The Author

Twila Jensen earned her master's degree in theology at Brewer Christian College and Graduate School. She serves as an adjunct professor and Director of Academic Operations at the University of Northwestern—St. Paul, a Christian institution. Twila married her high school sweetheart more than twenty-five years ago; the two have three sons together.

Twila Jensen, whose first name comes from the Hebrew word meaning "to pray" (*tefilah*), has a passion for the personal transformation that springs from communion with God through prayer and studying scripture. She is also the author of *Wings of Eagles*, a devotional book about finding God in difficult circumstances.

Printed in the United States
By Bookmasters